Wolfgang Lauber

TROPICAL ARCHITECTURE

Sustainable and Humane Building in Africa, Latin America and South-East Asia

with contributions by
Peter Cheret, Klaus Ferstl and Eckhart Ribbeck

Prestel
Munich · Berlin · London · New York

Contents

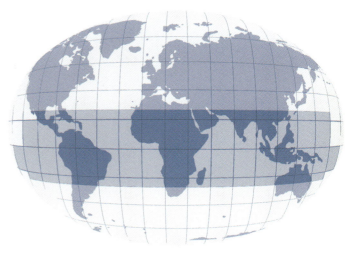

An Introduction to the World of the Tropics

A building from the German colonial period in southern Cameroon serves as a good example of a well-ventilated structure in the hot and humid climate zone through open, natural ventilation.

Traditional Dogon architecture on the cliffs of Bandiagara in Mali (left) and an extension of a city in the humid savannah of Cameroon (below).

Building in the Tropics means a confrontation in terms of construction and function with extreme climatic conditions. The architect and builder in moderate climatic zones combats cold and damp by using insulated external walls, avoiding cold bridges and through the development of technologically sophisticated heating systems.

The architect in the Tropics must, by contrast, battle against heat, strong solar radiation, high levels of air humidity and torrential rainfall and, in addition, develop methods of building that offer users comfortable spaces without requiring mechanical cooling systems, which from an ecological viewpoint are anyhow senseless as they use six times as much energy as space heating that today is still generally produced from primary energy sources.

The traditional vernacular architecture of the Tropics has, over a long period of time, developed intelligent building forms, sequences of spaces and construction methods for living and working, as well as for the cultural and religious ceremonies of societies that are principally agrarian in nature.

The encounter with European civilisation through colonisation led to a collapse of traditional cultural forms in the tropical climatic zones of the so-called Third World and to changes in the way of life there. For centuries, the building tasks had remained the same, shaped by the continuity of the circumstances of life in a traditional society.

Building forms and methods, clothing and objects of daily use, education and communication, family and religion, art forms and ornament, transport and types of trade, handcrafts and industrial production – all experienced profound change. Improvements in terms of nutrition and hygiene and the successful battle against major diseases (epidemics) led to a marked growth in population. Both the nature and extent of the tasks faced by tropical architecture in modern times are unparalleled in history.

After 1900, and following the course of developments in 19th-century Europe, the population began to increase substantially. At the same time, much like in Europe, a change also took place in the

percentages of the populat on living in towns and in the country. The increase in population, however, mostly affected the towns. In view of the population explosion in the tropical countries of the Third World we must develop a new, climatically appropriate and ecologically oriented architecture for 'normal' building tasks such as housing, schools, health care, administration and office buildings. This architecture should reflect our concern about a global environmental catastrophe and create liveable spaces for those who use it. Hygiene is also an important consideration here, for in hot tropical climates air-conditioning systems are often not adequately serviced and become polluted, leading to serious respiratory illnesses (such as the SARS epidemic). In the decades to come, the major building tasks of the so-called First World will gradually shift to the so-called Third World.

Of the present world population of 6 thousand million (statistics in 2004), 5 thousand million live in the Third World. In the future, the population explosion in these emerging countries will demand the construction of housing, administration, cultural and social buildings – requirements that it will be impossible to meet using old, outdated European models.

At the outset of the 20th century, 10 per cent of the world population lived in the cities. In 2000, around 50 per cent of the world population lived in the cities. By 2025, the number of city dwellers could reach 5 thousand million. In 1950, only New York and London had over 8 million inhabitants. Today there are 22 megalopolises of this size. Every hour there are:

+ 60 inhabitants in Manila
+ 47 inhabitants in Delhi
+ 21 inhabitants in Lagos
+ 12 inhabitants in London
+ 9 inhabitants in New York
+ 2 inhabitants in Paris

Of the 33 megalopolises predicted for 2015, 27 will be located in the most underdeveloped countries, including 19 in Asia.

Since many countries in the Tropics gained their independence important investments have been made there over the last 50 years in improving the infrastructure, especially transport, supplies, urban planning and housing, as well as public buildings for education, communal functions, administration and culture. However, the majority of the buildings show only a minimal response in terms of architecture and construction to the special conditions of the tropical climate and reveal little effort to develop ecological solutions.

It is regrettable that many examples reflect an uncritical reception of modern European settlement and building forms without taking into consideration the special climatic and social conditions of the tropical world.

Above all in the conurbations of the major cities of the Third World, administration buildings and

Traditional bamboo architecture with a grass roof alongside a corrugated-iron shack; new cheaply manufactured industrial goods from Asia are replacing traditional products.

Street market in Bamako, Mali (top). Improvements in the availability of medical treatment and services, along with increased agricultural productivity due to better cultivation methods and new kinds of grains and fruits, have contributed considerably to the growth in populations and cities, for example Bangkok (right).

housing blocks offer examples of a questionable use of technical cooling or heating systems, whose energy requirements amount to 40–50 per cent of the total energy consumption and which are met by non-renewable fossil fuels. Worldwide, this amounts in one year to a quantity of energy that took one million years to produce in the form of fossil fuel. This ecological aspect of sustainable architecture should be considered not only regionally in terms of the world of the Tropics but also globally out of a sense of responsibility for our environment.

At the international environment conference 'Rio + 10' held in Johannesburg, South Africa, in 2002, delegates underlined the significant role played by climatically appropriate, ecological building in promoting sustainable development. Through working out regional solutions for the climatic problems of a location, architecture can arrive at independent forms of expression and in this way make an individual contribution to a country's culture.

Against the background of the negative situation of 'normal' contemporary building in the Tropics,

a return to the 1,000-year-old building experience of traditional vernacular architecture in the Tropics could represent an important and exemplary aid in the sense of 'learning from our forefathers'.

This book concentrates on distilling the principles of climatically appropriate building in the Tropics as regards town planning, architecture and spatial design, building materials and building physics. The results are based on research work carried out over the past twenty years at the University of Applied Sciences in Constance and the University of Stuttgart, Germany.

A new urban expansion area (top) in Cameroon: unsuitable house types that lead to a loss of comfort through insufficient privacy towards the public road and inadequate protection from the sun.

A hotel in Togo with wrong east-west orientation leading to high cooling costs (centre left); and an apartment building in Brazil that is badly climatised resulting in the need for air-conditioning (centre right). A traditional meeting hall in Cameroon utilising natural cooling principles (right).

The urban expansion of Timbuktu (opposite page, top): a negative example with streets that are too wide and which fan out towards the sand-bearing Harmattan wind (north-east trade wind), causing the inner city to fill up with sand.

Defining the Climatic Zones

The tropical rainforest on the coast of Togo

The Tropics are defined by three climatic zones: hot and humid (top); hot and dry (centre); and, towards the edges of the tropical climatic zone, desert (bottom).

The world of the Tropics

The tropical belt of the earth is characterised by extremes in both geographical and meteorological terms. The highest mountains with numerous active volcanoes, the longest rivers with the highest water-falls and the largest deserts all lie in the Tropics. Equally extreme are the climatic conditions confronting architects and builders in the Tropics who want to design and construct buildings that create comfortable spaces for the users.

The strong solar radiation causes high temperatures in the dry zones during the summer; by contrast, the winter nights are cold nights.

In the humid zones the temperature remains constantly high with little difference between day and night, which, combined with high levels of humidity and little air movement, leads to a barely tolerable climate. Torrential rainfall and tropical cyclones require special construction methods to stabilise buildings.

Tropical storms develop primarily in the calm zones in the equatorial area, from where they move north or south, accompanied by high wind speeds and heavy, rain-driven rainfall.

The word 'tropics' is derived from the Greek word *tropikos* (referring to the apparent turning of the sun at the solstice). Today, by 'tropical zones' we mean the regions between latitude 23°26' north and south of the equator. The northern tropic is the Tropic of Cancer, where the sun is directly overhead on 22 June; the southern tropic is the Tropic of Capricorn, where on 23 December the sun stands directly overhead. To the north or south of the Tropics the sun is never directly overhead.

Climatic and geographic circumstances create environmental conditions that can be separated into two broad categories:

1. Warm, humid regions with tropical rainforests, monsoon regions and humid savannahs on the equator

2. Hot, dry regions of the deserts, semi-deserts, steppes and dry savannahs, close to the two tropics.

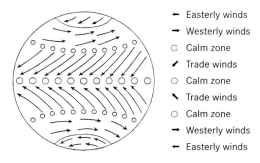

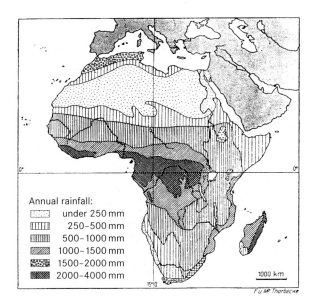

Annual rainfall:
- under 250 mm
- 250–500 mm
- 500–1000 mm
- 1000–1500 mm
- 1500–2000 mm
- 2000–4000 mm

1000 km

Global air movement (above) and the tropical zone in terms of annual precipitation, using the continent of Africa as an example (right)

The hot and humid climatic zones of the rainforest

In contrast to open savannahs, tropical rainforests are defined by the dense growth of jungle that offers protection to man and animals.

The hot and humid climate is influenced by the low pressure area of the calm zones with little air movement, frequent dense cloud cover with diffuse sunshine, and a rainy period several months long, extending from June to October, when heavy rainfall results in abundant surface and ground water. Particularly in south-eastern Asia, the summer monsoon, which brings the heaviest rainfall in the Tropics and the greatest frequency of tropical storms, exerts a strong influence on the climate. Within wooded areas individual clearings for settlements can be made on y by slashing and burning down trees or by extensive felling and by laying bush fires every year to prevent regrowth.

The rainforest zone with its luxuriant vegetation determines the ecological behaviour of the people living there who must regularly free their cultivated and settlement areas from the naturally occurring overgrowth.

The traditional building materials of the rainforest are timber, bamboo and grass or palm fibres. They are used in lightweight rod structures or, in combination with clay, as taipa building systems

Warm and humid regions

- ► Region: *c.* 15° north and south of the equator (Central Africa)
- ► Rainforest regions: on the coasts and in the equatorial lowlands
- ► Earth: red or brown
- ► Vegetation: impenetrable undergrowth, tall trees (jungle), extremely wet ground, high groundwater table
- ► Yearly differences: slight
  Northern hemisphere:
      Coolest months: December/January
      Warmest months: April–August, with
      greatest amount of precipitation

Southern hemisphere:
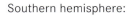
Coolest months: April–July
Warmest months: October–February,
with greatest amount of precipitation
► Low pressure area resulting in:
► cloudy and humid conditions throughout the year
► moderate to high amounts of solar radiation
depending on cloud formation
► temperature with slight variations: 31°C (annual
average) difference between day and night
(5° to 7°C)
► high rainfall
► Air movement: one or two dominant wind
directions, in the case of stormy rainfall up to
wind force 6 and more
► Climate: difficult to tolerate
Low evaporation of perspiration due to the
high level of air humidity and only slight air
movement.
Storms occur on 120–140 days of the year.
High risk of decay of organic building materials
and of rust in the case of metals

A plantation and a fisherman's house on stilts (above) in
a dangerous flooding area on the Amazon River, Brazil

The thick vegetation of the rainforest, in this case in southern
Cameroon, is typical for the hot and humid climate zone
(opposite page).

20

Humid savannah areas
- ► Rainy forests and bush
- ► Verdant landscape, even during the dry period
- ► Tall trees with deep roots. High soil humidity during the rainy period which reduces rapidly afterwards
- ► 2 seasons: mostly hot and dry, partly warm and humid

  Northern hemisphere:

  November–February: cool, March–June: hot, June–September: rainy

  Southern hemisphere:

  June–September: cool, October–January: hot, December–March: rainy

  These periods can move considerably (by up to 2 to 3 months)
- ► Partly blue skies during the rainy season with thundercloud formation
- ► Moderate to high levels of solar radiation
- ► Temperature: 26°C–32°C (yearly average during the day), at night it cools down to 18°C–20°C.
- ► Precipitation: little or no rainfall during the dry period 1,200–1,900 mm annually
- ► Medium air pressure
- ► Air humidity: high, 30–50% during the dry period, 55–100% during the rainy season
- ► Intense heat in the interior of the continent towards the end of the dry period as the constant north-east wind abates
- ► Expansion and shrinking of hygroscopic materials due to the great differences in air humidity between the dry and rainy seasons

Typical examples of humid savannah areas: Bamako in Mali (top left, opposite page bottom) and a single compound in the grasslands of Cameroon (opposite page top).

Examples of the hot and dry climatic zone of
the savannah: a traditional Dogon village in Mali
and a village in northern Cameroon

22

The dry and hot climatic zone of the savannah

In sharp contrast to the closed impenetrable rainforest, the savannah is characterised by openness. Freestanding trees scattered across open grass plains offer an overview and a feeling of expanse. The openness of the savannah means that it does not offer the protection of the rainforest and that man and animals are completely exposed there. The climate is marked by high-pressure weather and strong solar radiation, dryness with low precipitation (which occurs during the short rainy season from July to September), significant difference in temperature between day and night and strong winds from the north-east in the winter months from December to January that bring with them the cold of the northern desert.

There is a great shortage of water, which is generally found only in a few depressions with deep wells that never dry up. The availability of water determines the location of settlements.

The fertile earth of the grain-growing areas profits from the short rainy season. Where there is a shortage of fertile earth, the settlements are moved to the topographical perimeter zones to preserve the maximum amount of cultivated land.

In the savannah, the farming people live together with nature and try to preserve natural resources. Clay is the building material of the savannah: it is widely available owing to the geological decomposition of the granite bed into clay, which combines with sand blown in, and is used to build solid structures. Timber is rare and must be transported a considerable distance.

Climate of the dry savannah

- ► Transitional areas from hot and humid to hot and arid zones: e. g. southern Sudan, Zimbabwe, Tanzania, Mali: steppe, bush, prairie, grassland
- ► Vegetation: high to extremely high grass, low thorny woods with individual trees (tamarisks, shea and karité trees among others), luxuriant growth during the rainy season, at other times dried grass and leafless bushes
- ► Three seasons: cool, hot, rainy
  Climate in the northern hemisphere:
  November–March: cool, May–September: hot, July–October: rainy
  Southern hemisphere:
  May–August: cool, September–March: hot, December–May: rainy. These periods can change by anything up to 2 months
- ► Clear blue skies after the rainy season, then the amount of dust in the air increases as a result of the trade wind and the Harmattan in Africa
- ► Moderate to high amounts of direct solar radiation
- ► Air humidity: 20–35% during the dry season, 55–95% during the rainy season
- ► High air pressure
- ► Wind: strong and constant (also during the night) from the north–east (trade wind), tends to die down towards the end of the dry season
- ► Expansion and shrinking of moisture-absorbent materials
- ► Temperatures: 26°C–35°C (yearly average)
  Cools down at night to between 5°C and 18°C
  Considerable temperature difference between day and night of c. 20°C due to irradiation into the clear night sky and lack of vegetation that might retain water and of large areas of water
- ► Daytime maximum c. 40°C March–April
  Night-time minimum c. 5°C December–January
- ► Precipitation: 500–700 mm annually

The climatic zone of the desert

Life in the dry, hot desert zones is marked by shortages of all kinds. The shortage of water and fertile ground, which exists only in the river valleys of the oases, means for the few oasis farmers and live-stock-herding nomads a minimum existence that must be wrested from harsh natural conditions
The climate is marked by strong solar radiation from clear skies due to the predominant high-pressure weather situation, which also causes a constant, strong north-east wind, at times in the form of a sandstorm, in the northern hemisphere and a south-east wind in the southern hemisphere. The nights cool down quickly under clear, starry skies. The extremely low air humidity is due to the high-pressure weather conditions and the low levels of precipitation. Rain occurs only a few weeks in the year.
The insight into an existence very different to our consumer society with its abundance of everything can lead us, from the security of our familiar surroundings, to think critically about our consumption-oriented lifestyle and about a new environmental awareness.

At the international environmental protection conference held in Johannesburg in August 2002, this aspect was emphasised, seeing as around 60 per cent of the energy used worldwide in building is required for heating and, above all, for cooling.
The architecture of the desert also illustrates the difference between European and African cultures in their philosophical approach to transience: our efforts concentrate on building things made of stone, concrete and steel to resist the ravages of time, our useful objects are made of pottery and stainless steel, and our grotesque gravestones of granite. Inhabitants of the desert are entirely different: they renovate their unbaked mud buildings in a yearly rhythm for as long as they are used. These structures require constant care and maintenance; if neglected, they decay rapidly and are restored to their original natural state (clay) by the destructive forces of erosion through rain and wind.
Clay is a wonderful building material: at the end of its useful life it leaves behind no permanent ruins, and in this respect architecture can be regarded as a sign of the transitoriness of our existence.

The climate of the desert regions

- ► Regions between 15° and 30° north and south of the equator, Sahara countries, the Near East, northern South America, northern China
- ► Deserts, semi-deserts
- ► Extremely dry, minimal amount of vegetation, sand, rock: brown or red due to iron ore content
- ► Strong reflection of light can be blinding, wind erosion (air-borne sand, wandering dunes)
- ► Groundwater table at great depth, a short period of plant growth follows the rainfall, the ground dries immediately after the rain ceases
- ► Only slight differences between the seasons
  Northern hemisphere:
  Coolest months: December–January, warmest months: May–September
  Southern hemisphere:
  Coolest months: June–July, warmest months: November–March
- ► Great intensity of light, clear skies, darkening of the skies during sandstorms
- ► Strong, direct solar radiation
- ► Air temperature in the shade rises quickly after sunrise to a daily maximum of between 43°C and 49°C
- ► At night, c. 20°C or locally lower (in December around freezing point)
- ► Light rainfall, for only a few weeks. Maximum precipitation: 250 mm annually
- ► High air pressure
- ► Wind movement: often strong, during the day from the north-east (northern hemisphere) or south-east (southern hemisphere), stronger than at night. Hot or warm wind, tornados and sandstorms

The climate is tolerable thanks to the low air humidity: between 15 and 25 per cent. The great temperature differences can cause damage to buildings

The city of Tichitt, Mauritania (opposite page), and the habitat of the camel-herding nomads in the Sahel (above) illustrate the climatic zone of the desert.

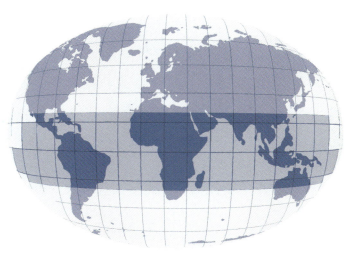

A Critical View of Present-day Building in the Tropics

A fully air-conditioned conference centre in Mali's capital, Bamako

A critical view of present-day building in the Tropics

Since gaining independence, the many tropical countries have made important investments over the last 50 years to improve the infrastructure, in particular in the areas of transport, supplies, urban planning and housing, as well as in public buildings for education, communal functions, administration and culture.

However, the majority of the buildings show only a minimal response in terms of architecture and construction to the special conditions of the tropical climate and reveal little effort to develop ecological solutions. It is regrettable that many examples reflect an uncritical reception of modern European settlement and building forms without taking into consideration the special climatic and social conditions of the tropical world.

A hotel in Lomé, Togo (top left): a fully air-conditioned glass building with very high energy expenditure for cooling necessitated by a disregard for the local climate, in that the facades are orientated towards the east and west. To run its air-conditioning system, this high-rise building requires 16 per cent of the entire electricity needs of Lomé, a city with a population of more than one million inhabitants.

A new bank building in Bamako, Mali (top right): the façades are inclined towards the sun on all sides so that the building heats up all day. This leads to high levels of energy consumption by the fully air-conditioned building.

An administration building and a cultural centre (bottom right and left) in Mali. The inappropriate building form (the inclined surfaces are turned towards the sun) creates interiors that are uncomfortable to use because of the excessive heat that builds up during the day.

"The use of numerous new techniques has allowed architecture to escape the restraints imposed by places and materials, indeed to liberate itself from them entirely. The result of this approach is the 'International Style'. For the first time in the history of architecture one sees identical buildings in almost all corners of the world. As it was those societies with the highest level of industrialisation that spread this style, it rapidly became a symbol of progress and wealth.

Such buildings either cause unacceptable running costs or are far more uncomfortable than an old building that is adapted to the climatic conditions could ever be. Viewed in this light, colonial architecture – and also traditional architecture – is today still highly instructive. The examination of their constructional and technical solutions is more valuable for architects in tropical regions than ever before. The optimal natural cross-ventilation of spaces and the protection against direct sunshine offered by walls are benefits easy to achieve using local materials. Thanks to the low costs of such solutions it is possible to offer more people dwellings that are better suited for living, which in itself represents significant social progress. If we turn to regional solutions for climatic problems we give our architecture the necessary natural basis. In architecture, as in all areas of human life, this is the expression of the culture of a country." (Nicolas Chambon, in *German Colonial Architecture in Togo*, 1990)

The gradual disappearance of traditional architectural forms in black Africa is an inevitable result of decisive social and economic changes. In many places, abandoned villages and buildings are an indication of the transition from a long-lasting traditional culture to a new era that is strongly influenced by the characteristics of our modern, Western way of life, although its suitability has yet to be proved.

A modern settlement in Yaounde, Cameroon (opposite page, top), that ignores the social needs of the future users by unquestioningly adopting European housing construction standards.
The lack of private courtyards, the stacked dwellings with undersized balconies, the lack of sun protection for the windows and the space-forming external walls lead to a loss of the comfort to which Africans were accustomed in their traditional houses. As a result, these dwellings must be electrically air-conditioned at a high cost if they are to be sold or let at all and not just allowed to degenerate into slums.

The US Embassy in Yaounde, Cameroon (opposite page, bottom), with high energy consumption caused by the air-conditioning appliances subsequently fitted to the windows. This is an example of false modernity in a building that fails to take into account regional climatic conditions.

A school in the dry savannah of Mali (top) – correctly oriented east-west and with sensibly designed façades with sun protection for the space-defining external classroom wall provided by the south-facing veranda placed in front of it.
Unfortunately, the same does not apply to the second classroom block standing to the south of the courtyard. For formal reasons (the two buildings are placed on either side of an axis of symmetry running through the schoolyard) it uses the same spatial concept – but mirrored. This means that the classrooms on the south side of the second block have no protection against the sun, as the veranda is to the north of the classrooms. Furthermore, the mono-pitch metal roof is inclined in the wrong direction – towards the south.

Rio de Janeiro is a fascinating metropolis embedded in a unique setting of bays and wooded mountains. Rio could today be one of the most beautiful cities in the world, as it still was in the 1940s, if unrestricted speculation by investors had not largely destroyed the urban space.

Only a few buildings show evidence of a climatically appropriate architecture that takes the hot, humid coastal climate into account. One example is the Sheraton Hotel. The cooling sea breezes in the morning and the offshore winds in the evening can ventilate the development along the coast and contribute to comfortable living conditions. Unfortunately, all the hotel bedrooms have electrical air-conditioning systems and hotel guests are thus unable to experience the tropical regional climate in the evening. This regrettable American approach is based on the wish to offer the guests of international hotel chains uniform conditions throughout the world.

The urban expansion of Rio de Janeiro (above) obstructs the natural ventilation of the city in much the same way that the buildings along the coast of Niterói (left) block the natural sea breezes.

The Sheraton Hotel (right) in Rio. This striking building is positioned correctly, at right angles to the beach and to the wooded mountain slope rising behind it.

The Museum of Contemporary Art (above) in Niterói by Oscar Niemeyer (1991) illustrates a climatically appropriate concept in that the façades are turned away from the sun.

The multi-storey apartment block (right) by Affonso Eduardo Reidey (1950): a maisonette-type apartment building with climatically appropriate detailing of the façades and cross-ventilation of the spaces that are higher than usual.

The majority of the housing blocks (opposite page) in Rio de Janeiro and even the PUC University (opposite, top) are air-conditioned artificially using high levels of energy consumption through individual air-conditioning boxes fixed to the windows. The knowledge that was once employed in traditional colonial architecture to cool living rooms has been largely lost and forgotten.

The correct east-west positioning of Affonso Eduardo Reidy's Museum of Modernism (opposite, bottom) in Rio de Janeiro provides natural ventilation for the new building (which has an open ground floor) and exploits local wind conditions on the coast to the front. The widely projecting roof, ventilated from below, shades the façades.

Architecture in South-East Asia and China

The new megacities in the south-east Asian economic area, such as Shanghai, attempt to solve the enormous pressure exerted by the influx of people from rural areas by stacking vertically. The American principle of the fully air-conditioned high-rise building for living and working is a suggestion that seems initially obvious, but one that has considerable disadvantages in the social area – such as flats in tower blocks that are unsuited for children and lack sufficient, easily accessible playing areas. In many new mass housing estates where the young migrant population is stacked vertically, the loss of the values of traditional living forms is lamentable. The high quality of life offered by the traditional courtyard-type house (despite its inadequacies in the area of sanitary facilities) with its consideration of human needs – such as the protection of the privacy of family life, the dignity of the individual,

and the provision of comfort during the different seasons – has, sadly, been lost.

Just as regrettable is the contemptuous treatment of the individual as shown in the layering of work-spaces in anonymous high-rise buildings. As they are completely air-conditioned, these buildings lack any natural relationship to the outside climate. In terms of energy policy, the waste of expensive primary energy to generate electricity for air-conditioning systems is appalling, especially when contrasted with the use of natural principles of cooling in the old colonial buildings with their alcoves and verandas placed in front of the main structure to provide shade. The exclusive use of technically-based concepts such as electrical air-conditioning systems, without considering natural principles of ventilation, leads to regular power cuts in the hot season as well as hygiene problems caused by the accumulation of dirt in the air-conditioning ducts.

View of the centre of Hong Kong (top right) and of the megacities Bangkok, Thailand (top left), and Shanghai, China (bottom)

The lack of urban concepts based on a response to the tropical climate and to the most basic of human needs, such as the protection of privacy, and a sense of security and comfort, turns large cities into urban nightmares.

Bangkok is today one of the most polluted cities in the tropical world. The shapeless and arbitrary stacking of living and working space in fully air-conditioned high-rise buildings reveals the utter helplessness of the town planners confronted with the needs of millions of people fleeing the country-side, who then cling to their hopeless dreams of a better life in the slums of the big cities.

Apartment blocks in the cities of Singapore and Hong Kong (above) with their energy-devouring individual air-conditioning appliances for every living room (right). A courtyard building in northern China (far right), where the private sequence of courtyards is screened from the access road by enclosing walls with an intimate entrance. The north-south orientation of the courtyards flanked by the dwellings protects against the cold north winds and ensures optimal sunshine for the east- and west-facing façades of the houses.

An Analysis of Traditional Architecture in the Tropics

Traditional architecture in the savannah of Mali

The hot, humid climatic zone of the rainforest and the coast

Traditional forms of settlement in the rainforest
The scattered settlement is the settlement form favoured by the farming population in the rainforest zone. This kind of development is made possible by the fertility of the soil and an adequate supply of water through rainfall and surface water. Unlike in the savannah it is not vital to preserve valuable cultivated land by concentrating buildings in less fertile areas. At topographically suitable locations periodic clearing of the woodland (extensive agriculture) allows the areas needed for the smallholders and their compounds to be laid out. Keeping the routes between the residential area and the cultivated farmland short makes it easier to farm the land. The centrally located villages are centres of administration, justice, markets and crafts and are built as administrative units on suitable, easily accessible sites such as plateaus or valleys that are cleared in major felling operations.

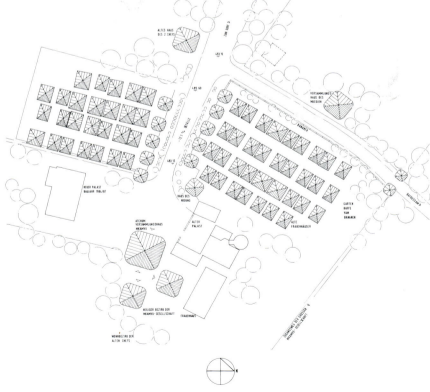

The palace complex of Bandjoun in Cameroon (above) shows an open development with broad street spaces, illustrated in the plan (right).

A pile-dwelling settlement (opposite page) in Benin. The large compound of Bafut, set in a woodland clearing, has a scattered settlement structure. The community protected itself against attack by fleeing into the impenetrable surrounding forest (bottom).

The scattered development of traditional individual compounds in the mountainous region of West Cameroon

A compound consists of a group of freestanding dwelling houses and storerooms in which an extended family lives together. This family is made up of the head of the family and his several wives, each of whom generally has between three and five children.

An example of traditional architecture in the mountainous region of West Cameroon

In earlier times, the birth rate was considerably higher, as was the infant mortality rate. Today, birth control is promoted by the state and a health care service is being developed through the erection of hospitals and health care centres, even in the most remote mountain villages.

Often, members of the older generation of a family, generally the father of the head of the clan and his wives, occasionally also relatives, live together with the young people. These elderly people are respected and integrated into the unit of the extended family. They help in processing the harvest, in cooking, and in raising the children.

The site plan of such a compound reveals an astonishing quality in the sensitivity with which individual areas are defined. The approach route always leads through a belt of crops such as cola nut trees, banana plantations, coffee bushes and yams to the entrance courtyard with its 'public' functions. This is where the head of the family, whose house 'guards' the entrance area, receives visitors.

From this open space, narrow routes or passageways lead between the corners of the dwelling houses to the 'private' areas that again are screened by lightweight woven fences made of bamboo cane and palms. These fences allow the cooling wind to pass through but provide a visual screen that creates a protected private area and, as they also allow sounds to pass through, nevertheless permit a feeling of community to develop.

The sequence of open and screened areas in a compound and the allocation of lush plantations to the small courtyards, which are generally closed on three sides, create a feeling of security and a pleasant domestic quality.

The interior of a dwelling house in Ebjunjbam, Oku, in Cameroon, built around 1920: woven bamboo walls, benches along the walls, beds, smoke extract above the hearth with a level used for smoking food.

Opposite page:
Stages involved in the construction of a typical house:
1 Plinth and foundations
2 Erection of the prefabricated wall elements in a single piece, made of three layers of bamboo, 3-5 cm in diameter
3 Attic storey, one prefabricated part
4 Four roof hips
5 Insertion of the hanging trusses and suspended floors

Typology and design of the rod-structure buildings

The free-standing dwelling house

Each traditional house within the compound of an extended family is inhabited by an adult. This can be either a man or one of his wives; the woman generally lives together with her small children. Each married woman has her own house and the different wives alternately visit the man in his own house.

The traditional houses generally consist of a single room that is subdivided only along the wall plane into niches by the use of shelves and lightweight screen walls.

The floor plan and size of a traditional house are generally determined by at least four beds that are usually positioned along two opposite walls. In a woman's house, the woman sleeps in one bed and the children in the other beds – sometimes two to four children in each bed.

The women cook on the hearth in the house; separate kitchens or kitchen huts are found only in the more recent clay buildings that often consist of several rooms in one house. Walls on both sides of the sliding entrance door screen the two beds standing with their heads against the entrance wall. The seating area and the central cooking hearth with a constantly burning fire form an inviting centre to the space.

The constant smoke means that the bamboo canes in the interior are covered with paint-like, shiny black soot. At places, long strands of soot hang from a bamboo ceiling that allows the smoke to pass through it. The smoke created by the permanent fire is used to cure or smoke meat, maize and beans. These foodstuffs are placed on a suspended ceiling over the hearth, just above head height. The disinfecting effect of the smoke means that the interior of the house is free of insects. Ritual wooden masks are also stored on the bamboo ceilings or on storage

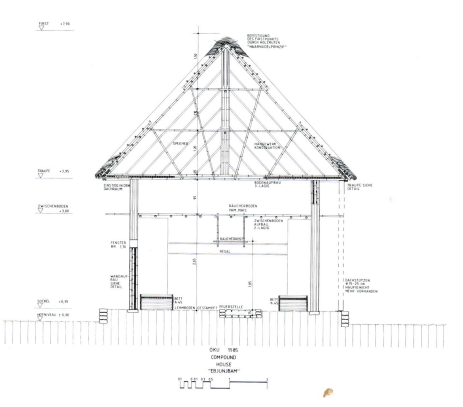

OKU 11·85
COMPOUND
HOUSE
"EBJUNJBAM"

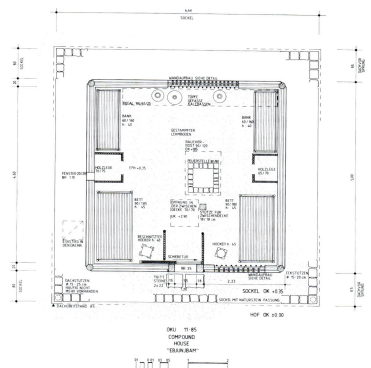

OKU 11·85
COMPOUND
HOUSE
"EBJUNJBAM"

areas above the hearth and the typically smoky smell they acquire serve to keep away termites. However, cancer of the respiratory system is widespread due to the carcinogenic carbon.

At either side of the space a tall stack of wood screens the two beds along the sidewall from each other. Here, as in the overall plan of the compound, considerable attention is paid to preserving a private space for the individual.

Opposite the entrance there is generally a shelf at head height to store cooking utensils, medicinal gourds and appliances. The length of two beds and the stacks of firewood determine the basic dimensions of a house, which vary between 4.6 to 6 metres square. The Tikar builders justify the square plan in structural terms, as it allows wall elements of the same size to be used on all four sides and, above all, permits them to use the clear structural form of a pyramid-shaped roof. Windows are rare, and where they do occur, they are generally in the form of small smoke extract openings. The walls are mostly closed up to door height.

The climatic protection of the living room is optimally solved. During the summer rainy season, cloud-bursts lead to flooding of the terrain. A clay plinth about 35 cm high lined with a protective edge of natural stone keeps the footings of the bamboo walls dry. The roof projects beyond the walls of the house by between 90 and 100 cm so that the eaves line is about 20 to 30 cm beyond the edge of the plinth, which also helps to protect the delicate bamboo walls from driving rain.

The tall attic space with its thick grass roofing forms an ideal heat buffer that is further improved by the void above the suspended ceiling.

The external walls are woven of five layers of bamboo canes, and the outside layer is often protected against wind and rain by a coat of clay. This outer skin favourably combines air permeability (ability to breathe) and thermal insulation properties.

Often, light screen walls of woven palm leaves are placed in the plane of the four timber columns carrying the roof. Owing to their low mass they do not heat up easily, provide shade and, like in the heat buffer formed by the attic, they also create a micro-climate that alleviates the effect of the heat on the interior. Even on hot, humid days the traditional bamboo house affords pleasant living conditions.

Traditional building forms and construction methods in the rainforest, illustrated using the example of the Palace of Bandjoun, Cameroon

The commonest method of construction in the rainforest is the lightweight rod structure as the rainforest offers sufficient hardwood of excellent quality that is resistant to termites and rot. Dense, tall growths of thick-stemmed bamboo are also to be found along the streams and in the marshy lowlands. Clay can be excavated only in the clearings and is therefore used mostly as infill material in the timber or bamboo frame in the manner of taipa construction. Raw plant materials for roof covering, such as grass or palm leaves, are becoming increasingly rare, owing to the intensive agricultural use of the land. To simplify the jointing of the rods in the traditionally prefabricated building elements, such as wall elements, ceilings or roofs, rod–structure buildings generally have rectangular plans.

The sizes of the spaces and the building forms of rodconstruction architecture are determined by the length of the building timber and of the bamboo cane, which in turn are restricted by the limited methods of unassisted transport in the rainforest (the use of a horse ard cart is generally impracticable). In addition, structurally suitable bamboo canes with a diameter of between five and six centimetres are generally available only in lengths of between five and six metres in the grassfields of Cameroon. The traditional builder constructs his spaces with only these locally available building materials and exploits their constructional potential in developing both the form of his buildings and the individual details of the design. These limited possibilities may explain the 'variety within an overall uniformity' of the Cameroon grassland buildings. In fact, the reduction of the room sizes to between 4 and 6 metres in length and width, which is also due to the lack of wide-spanning roof structures such as timber trusses, leads to a chain-like succession of single-storey spaces.

The tropical climate, with its high level of humidity, low movement of air and differences in temperature between day and night, is optimally dealt with in the traditional sequence of spaces. The external walls are closed, with only few openings for a door and smoke extraction, as well as cross-ventilation. Frequently, 'house-within-a-house' plans in the sense of a reduit offer additional climatic protection, often even further improved by a loggia running around all sides with mat walls forming *brise-soleils* that allow air to pass through.

The main internal space is enclosed by solid walls infilled with clay that modify the climate as they are protected against heating up by a lightweight veranda 'buffer' placed in front of them. The deep overhangs of the roof and the row of columns in front increase protection from the sun and keep the sensitive, light, translucent, woven bamboo walls from becoming wet during the heavy rain showers in the rainy season: this type of structure provided a model for the colonial buildings of the nineteenth century. The large, generally somewhat dark interior measuring about 100 square metres in floor area is lit from a roof light at the top that can be covered up. The open nature of the development allows open spaces, residential courtyards and routes to be well ventilated by the gentle air movement that is typical of the rainforest climate.

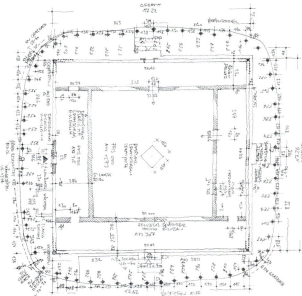

A row of timber columns in front and lightweight woven sun-screens provide shade for the core containing the living room while translucent walls allow cross-ventilation of the interior.

The palace of Big Babanki in Cameroon

This palace in the grasslands is one of the best-preserved traditional palace complexes. It illustrates many aspects of the old additive courtyard system with its horizontal system of escape routes that were a typical feature of large, historic palace complexes. In addition, the sacred Achum building, the residence of the king, forms the dominant centre of the entire complex.

The escape route system is a basic response to the many dangers that the king was exposed to in former times:

► The bamboo buildings, with their soot-lined interiors, posed a permanent fire risk, as the fire in the central hearth was kept burning both day and night and sparks from these fires could very quickly lead to a conflagration in the entire palace complex.

► In former times, tribal rivalries, disputes over succession to the throne and attacks by marauding, migratory bands were commonplace. They threatened the life of the king, which was of great importance for the farming community. He was the guardian of morals and order, the representative of religious belief and a unifying leader of a society of individual compounds that was often split by internal disputes.

► The escape route system also ensured the family life of the king a degree of privacy, as the individual women's courtyards bordered separately on the Achum, the dwelling of the king. Thus, one woman could enter the residence of the king unobserved by the others.

The various entrances and exits, in conjunction with a number of 'dead ends' within the building and the separation of the outdoor space of the Achum by fences covered with planting, provided a sophisticated system of horizontal escape routes that enabled the Fon to flee from danger via the women's courtyards into the surrounding bush.

The dense growth of the 'impenetrable' rainforest – accessible only by paths that are constantly kept clear or, in more recent times, by narrow roads – offers protection and reduces the risk of attack. In historic times, a well-developed surveillance system based on drum signals that could be heard over a distance of several kilometres provided early warning for the inhabitants of the individual compounds and the villages. In recent times, this system has been improved by modern forms of communication, such as radio and television. The narrow paths through the dense undergrowth that were difficult for horses to negotiate, and where large numbers of hostile foot soldiers were able to proceed only in single file, could be easily defended from the bush by means of ambush. In the case of attack by a numerically superior enemy, as occurred during the migration of entire tribes and which led to extensive ethnic changes in the rainforest until well into the 19th century, the locals' only option was flight into the surrounding rainforest, as their lightweight, permeable bamboo and wooden stick buildings could be easily destroyed or burnt down and thus offered little protection.

Flight rather than resistance or defence is therefore the typical approach of peoples in densely wooded areas. This explains the lack of fortified settlements there. The same approach is also illustrated in the plans of the compounds and palaces: openness and permeability rather than seclusion and enclosure are their principal forms of architectural expression.

The palace of Big Babanki (above) in Cameroon; the floor plan of the palace (right); and an illustration of the escape route system (far right) for the Fon through the women's private courtyards into the dense surrounding forest

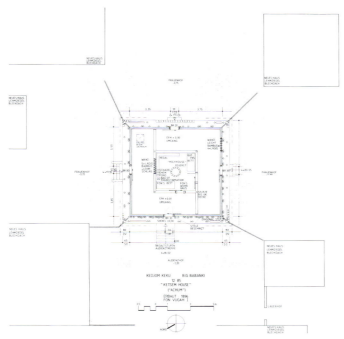

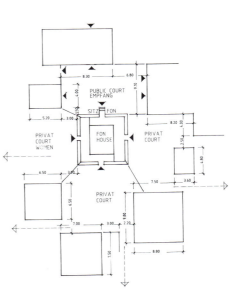

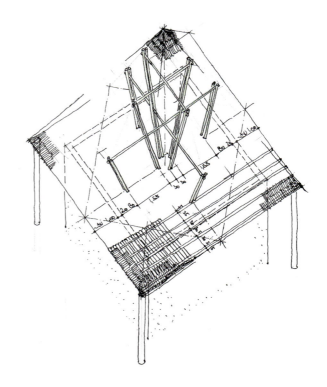

The traditional rod construction method and its influence on the form of bamboo buildings

Bamboo buildings are ecological in the best sense of the word. The scattered settlement pattern allows the natural forest to continue to grow between the individual compounds with large areas of bamboo along the numerous streams in the rainy mountainous area. This natural and sustainable building material with thicknesses of three to five centimetres and lengths of up to six metres is prepared on the building site of each particular building. As a first measure, a square plinth is built on the levelled and terraced sloping site using clay (earth) and natural stone, both of which are both widely available in the surrounding area.

The bamboo buildings are prefabricated on site. In this sense they correspond to the most recent European production techniques that try to avoid the expensive transport of large building elements over long distances. The erection of small lightweight uniform building elements on the site reduces the cost of building. The principle of the cube on a square plan, using uniform wall and roof elements

both shortens and simplifies the prefabrication process. The four panels forming the external walls and the four triangular-shaped roof trusses are erected on site and are made of between three and five layers of bamboo canes without the use of metal connections (nails, screws, etc.) Only bamboo pins and bands made of palm leaves are used to weave together the various layers of mats. Together with four corner piers to improve stability, the wall elements are raised into position and lined up at right angles – following Pythagoras' rule – with the help of woven plant ties (bands). The prefabricated roof is then placed on the external walls and connected to them by the building team. The free-standing external corner columns are placed in position before the four prefabricated roof trusses are raised into place. The internal rod structure – an ingenious, hanging, truss-like structure that resembles a piece of engineering – is then integrated.

The next step is to cover the roof with bent bunches of grasses inserted between horizontal roofing battens. When they are moistened the bent stems straighten out and swell, thus producing a dense

The intelligent rod-structure system (opposite page) of the Cameroon grasslands, with its insulating double-shell roof and lightweight covering of grass, forms a buffer zone for the living area constructed of bamboo canes below (as shown in the isometric view).

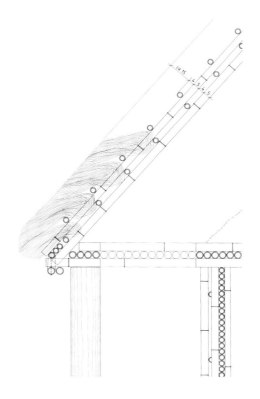

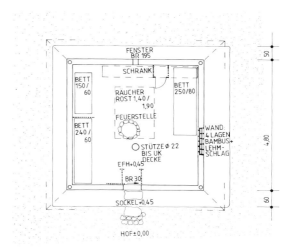

form of roof cover on the steeply sloping roof, which has pitch of about 45°.

Structurally, the danger of the building lifting during the rare heavy winds is avoided by the weight of the grass roof, which becomes heavy through rain during thunderstorms, as well as of the load of maize stored in the roof space and on a suspended smoking floor built of bamboo cane that is inserted later, along with the furniture.

The reduction of weight and the standardised junction details require a minimum of material and labour.

Building a house

The intact community of a compound or village is an important sociological aspect in the construction of a house. A house is built in only a few days through the joint efforts of many friends and neighbours, according to the principle of social, neighbourly assistance. The costs amount to only a few hundred dollars, as the material can be found for free in the neighbouring woods and only the meals for the building team have to be paid for.

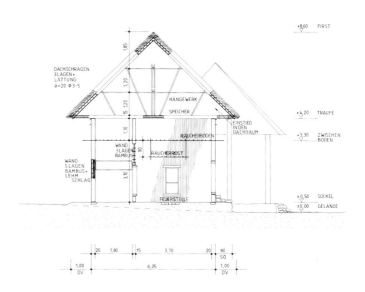

The hot and humid climate of the African coastal regions, taking Togo as an example

The climate is marked by high humidity and a predominant sea wind from the south-west. The structure of the settlements and the buildings takes these climatic factors into account, as is shown in the openness of the development, which resembles the settle ments in the wet, mountainous region of Cameroon.

The buildings are built in an open manner often with only an insulating grass roof with deep projecting eaves as protection from heavy summer rain. Visual protection is afforded by lightweight walls made of matting that allow the cooling sea breezes to pass through. Plant materials such as bamboo cane, grass mats and palm-leaf pan cles provide lightweight spatial shells that do not heat up in the daytime heat but afford pleasant climatic conditions in the evenings.

The open settlement form of the pile-dwelling fishing village (above) on Lake Ganvié, Benin, on the eastern border of Togo.

The lightweight external walls made of woven matting allow the living spaces to be ventilated by the fresh, lake breeze. The living areas are protected from the sun by insulating grass roofs (opposite page, top).

A large, grass-covered bamboo roof of an assembly hall with deep projecting eaves and overhangs – allowing winds to pass through easily, checked by only a few screen walls (opposite page, bottom).

54

A school built using the traditional wood and bamboo construction system

The building is correctly positioned east-west, which means that the light insulating grass roof with a deep overhang on the south side provides pleasant shade for the main space. The tall, open gables allow the dominant east wind to flow through the classroom.

By contrast, the new, neighbouring school is also positioned correctly in an east-west direction and has open classrooms that can be ventilated north-south, but the roof projections are too shallow to provide sufficient shade. A further point of criticism is that the structure is built of concrete and not of sand-cement blocks, which offer greater insulation. With such positive and negative examples directly beside each other, the 'loss of tradition' and of the wealth of experience of vernacular architecture is made particularly clear and contrasts sharply with 'official architecture', much to the latter's disadvantage.

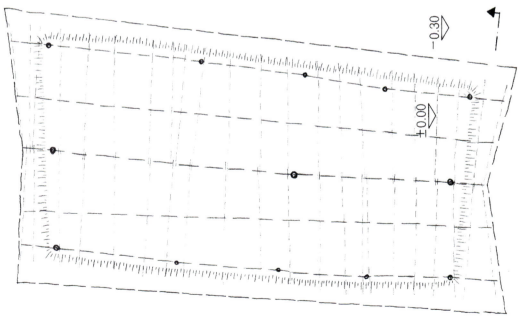

The old school opposite the new one (above) and a ground plan of the structure (right)

An open, cross-ventilated meeting hall (opposite page, top), shaded from the sun and based on a climatically-sensible spatial concept, and with a suitable choice of building materials for the insulating, grass-covered, lightweight bamboo roof. An open, freestanding kitchen provides pleasant working conditions thanks to cross-ventilation and extraction of fumes through a transparent, lightweight screen wall made of split bamboo canes.

The hot and humid climatic zone of the South-East Asian coastal regions

Traditional architecture in this region is influenced by the difficult climate with its high levels of humidity, little movement of air in the interior and light sea breezes along the coasts, as well as by constant high temperatures both day and night. Frequent tropical typhoons with heavy rainfall represent a serious problem for the construction of buildings during the monsoon summer. The settlements have an open permeable structure that, in conjunction with dense vegetation, provides a tolerable micro-climate in residential areas.

The typology of the buildings is marked by adaptation to the climate revealed in the raising of the buildings to allow the living spaces on the open, upper floor to be better cooled by the flow of the breeze, as air movement at ground-floor level is restricted by the low bushes that often grow there. This raising of the buildings also protects the inhabitants during the frequent floods that occur in the rainy season, as well as from the heavy monsoon rains and tsunami waves. The construction of the buildings using lightweight materials, such as bamboo cane, permeable woven mats made of plant-based materials and deep roof projections to provide protection from the sun and the rain, resemble in many aspects the climatically responsive solutions encountered in the architecture of the Cameroon rainforest.

Openness and lightness are the architectural mode of expression of this architecture e's intelligent response to a most difficult climate.

Houses of the Karo Batak (above) in northern Sumatra in a photograph of 1880

Opposite page: a building raised on stilts (top) in the Gulf of Papua, as illustrated in *Duperrey's Voyage of the Coquille*, (1821); photos of fishermen's villages (far left) on the coast of Sumatra, and of the King's palace in Minang Kaban (right).

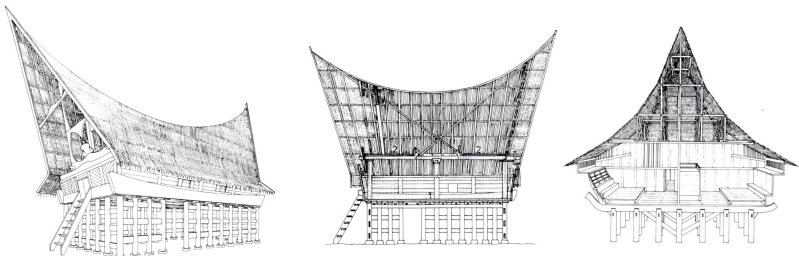

Houses in Nias, on Lake Toba, in Indonesia (external view and section). The elevated timber rod structures protect the living spaces from the effects of flooding and from soaking during the rainy season, as well as from tsunami waves. The raised living spaces on the first and second floors are better ventilated, as the coastal winds blow more strongly above ground level. Open verandas in front protect the living spaces from the sun and provide increased comfort.

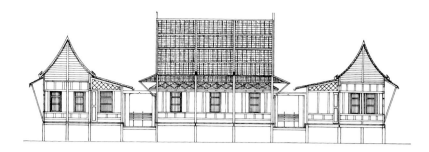

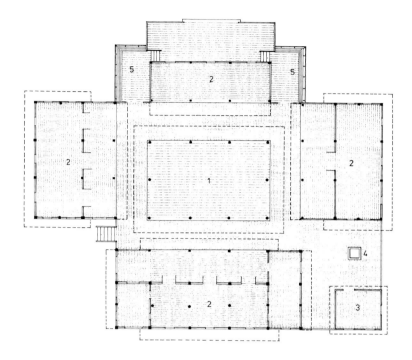

House in Aynthya, Thailand

In this example, the structure is raised on struts to protect it during the floods in the rainy season. The position of the individual buildings around an open, roofed communal space does not impede the movement of the wind and creates a wonderful domestic quality for an extended family consisting of twelve members, whose individual privacy is preserved in their living rooms and bedrooms.

At the same time, the central communal space creates a protected central area for family life. Even functional problems, such as those caused by Thai cuisine, whose preparation creates a considerable amount of fumes and smoke, are taken into account by the lateral position of the kitchen and the well allotted to it.

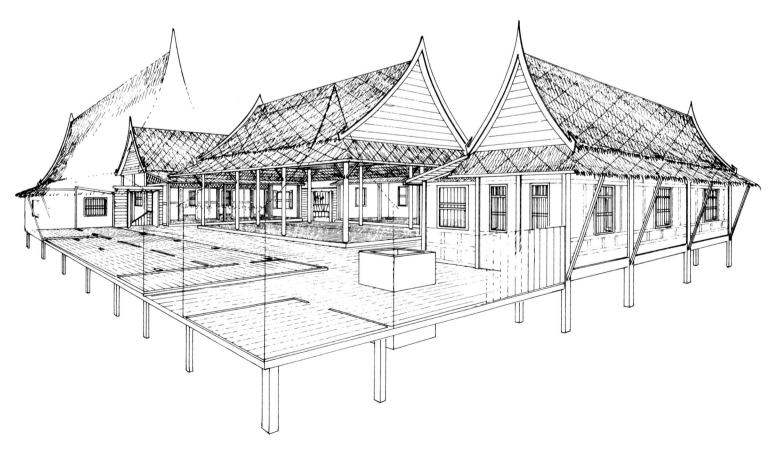

The traditional architecture of the savannah, using the West African countries of Mali and Togo as examples

In contrast to the dense impenetrable rainforest, the savannah is characterised by openness. The scattered vegetation, with single, free-standing trees and wide grass plains, offers an overview and creates a feeling of expanse. As a result of its openness the savannah does not offer the same protection as the rainforest; here, man and animals are completely exposed.

The climate is marked by high-pressure weather conditions with strong solar radiation and dryness with little precipitation. Rain occurs mostly in the short rainy season between July and September. Other characteristics of the climate are considerable differences between day and night time temperatures, a strong wind from the north-east, and the so-called trade wind of the high-pressure zone, which during the winter months brings with it the cold from the northern deserts.

The scarcity of water, which is generally found only in a few hollows with deep wells that never dry up, is the main factor in determining the location of the settlements. The fertile earth in the grain-growing areas benefits from the short rainy season. Where fertile ground is scarce, the settlements are moved to the topographical perimeter zones to preserve the maximum amount of cultivated land.

Clay is the principal building material of the savannah. It is widely available owing to the geological decomposition of the granite bed into clay, which combines with sand blown in by the wind, and is used to build massive structures. Timber, on the other hand, is rare and must be transported a considerable distance.

A baobab (top), the typical tree of the savannah in Dogon country, Mali (right).

Traditional forms of settlement in the savannah

The traditional settlement form of the farming peoples on the open savannah is the compact, closed village on the plain, in the mountains or on the rocky slopes. The defence works are formed like a city wall, using storage buildings placed close together or clay walls with only a few openings which, like historic city gates, are easy to defend. The reason for this traditional protected settlement form is to be found primarily in the unprotected open nature of the savannah. For attackers, in historic times often troops on horseback and slave hunters, such a settlement was easily recognisable and an obvious target to attack. Unlike the inhabitants of the rainforest, who could quickly disappear, the members of the village community could not save themselves by fleeing through the open and exposed savannah. The only option was to defend themselves behind the protective walls of the village. In addition, cleverly designed obstacles and narrowings were incorporated in the entrance areas as protection against attackers.

A climatic reason for the compact, vertical development of the villages and towns is the shade provided by tall buildings in the narrow lanes and squares and the barrier offered to sand and dust-carrying winds by the winding layout of the narrow routes.

The compact village settlement form also conserves fertile ground used for the growing of grain and vegetables. In contrast to the farming peoples of the humid and fertile rainforest, the inhabitants of the dry savannah are tied to the few places where groundwater is available. The compact settlement is a logical solution that offers short routes from the few water sources to the dwelling compounds and the artificially irrigated areas under cultivation.

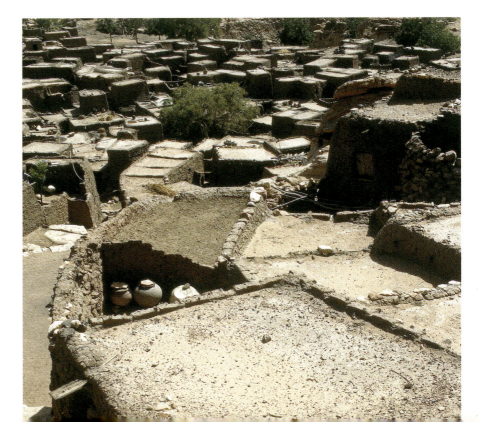

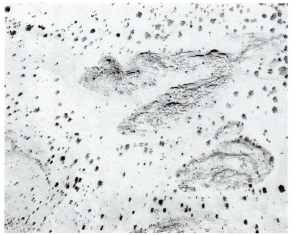

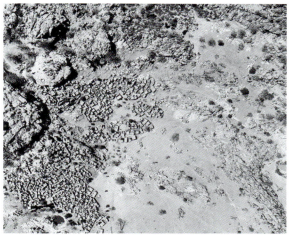

The densely built-up summit of a western defensive village (top) located on a table-top mountain above the fertile plain, and aerial views of the settlements (above and right). Climatic protection against sand and dust is offered by the winding layout of the routes leading to and through the settlements.

The lively square (bottom) of a defensive Dogon village on a
western table-top mountain and the urban sequence of lanes
and open spaces with entrances to the high town houses (right).

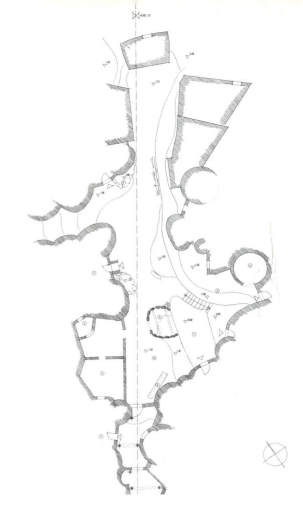

64   The traditional settlements of the Dogon had remarkable urban qualities: fine, open spaces lined by
town houses several storeys high. The communal
buildings for the meetings of the local council also
stood here, under the shade of large trees. There is
an intelligent transition from a communicative, public quality in the lanes and open spaces to a private
sphere in the sheltered internal courtyards and on
terraces shielded from outside view. A shaded lane
expands to provide a space for the communal work
of the women.

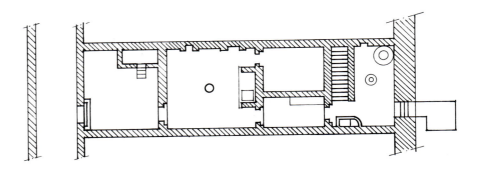

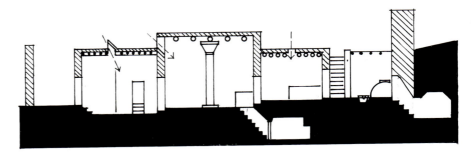

On the typology of the core house with an internal 'reduit' zone

The dry, hot climate of the savannah necessitates protection against the daytime heat in summer, when temperatures can rise to 45°C, and against the cold during the cool winter months with night-time temperatures around freezing point.
A solution to this problem is provided by an internal core of living spaces that is protected by a surrounding ring of buffer spaces.
This traditional building type has parallels to the termites' nests, into which the insects withdraw during extreme conditions outside.
The traditional core house with an internal protected 'reduit' zone offers the inhabitants optimum protection against the daytime heat and the cold at night. It is particularly those core houses with 'stacked' levels several storeys high and which require only a relatively small site area that are particularly suitable for uneven terrain and dense, compact settlements in which the buildings lie along narrow lanes and access streets.
The lighting and ventilation of the external buffer spaces arranged around the core demand that the building be free-standing on a lane or open site. The problem of lighting the internal core spaces is traditionally solved by roof lights or light wells.
This house type was developed thousands of years ago throughout the dry, hot climatic zone of the savannah, as the example of a terrace town house in Thebes from the time of the New Egyptian Empire shows.
This principle probably reached Europe via Greek and Roman culture, where it was further developed by the Romans in the form of the domed building that provided a model for Andrea Palladio's Villa Rotonda dating from 1570. This excellent example of the 'reduit' type has a central living hall protected by the surrounding bedrooms and ancillary spaces, and it is ventilated and lighted through a central opening providing a soft light.

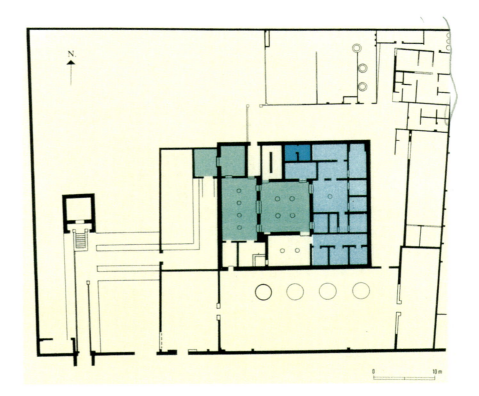

The plan of an Egyptian terrace town house (top right) from the 2nd millennium BC shows a sequence of spaces leading from the hall, located directly next to the lane, to the central living area / hall with a roof light for the internal zone. The bedroom with a roof light faces onto the courtyard, which also ventilates the kitchen (with its cool rock cellar for foodstuffs) and helps to extract cooking smells and fumes. The roof terrace was used as a sleeping area during balmy summer nights and for drying crops.

The core house (bottom) of an Egyptian notable during the reign of Tutmosis I, 2000 BC. The dwelling house with office/reception rooms lies in a walled garden with private rooms at the rear.

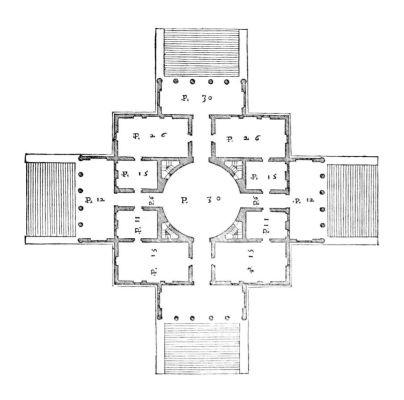

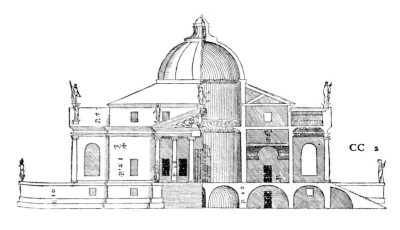

67

Andrea Palladio's Villa Rotonda (top left and right) in Northern Italy, 1570, demonstrates the principle of the central 'reduit' space used for the living area, lit and ventilated by an opening at the top of the cupola. The surrounding bedrooms and service spaces serve as buffers that protect the central space.
The porticoes built in front of the entrances offer shade and protection against the wind.

A traditional three-storey dwelling house of the western Dogon plateau with its organic, cellular floor plan (bottom). The 'reduit' principle with internal, climatically protected living rooms, and sleeping quarters with external 'buffer spaces' is formed by store-rooms and grain stores.

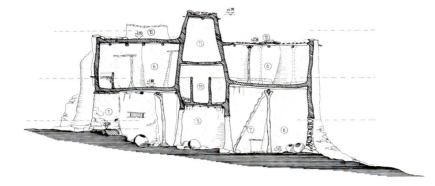

A traditional Dogon house in section and plan. The 'reduit' princi- ple with external 'buffer spaces' formed by the storerooms, grain store and kitchen

1 Entrance
2 Access to grain store on upper floor
3 Cooking
4 Seating area
5 Larder
6 Sleeping area on upper floor
7 Washing, toilet
8 Stables
9 Storage space
10 Terraces
11 Grain store

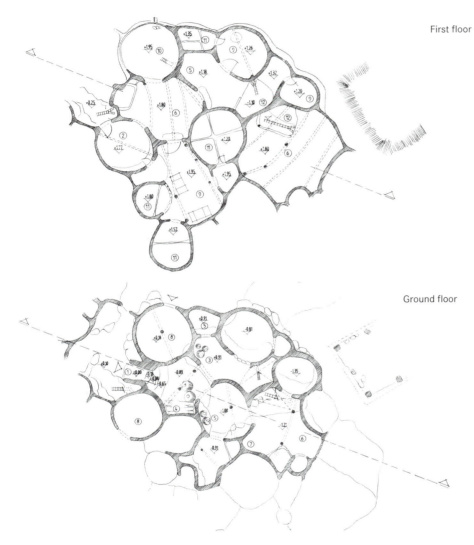

First floor

Ground floor

The traditional clay-built core house of the Dogon

In the savannah, massive clay construction is the most ecologically sensible way of creating climati- cally pleasant spaces.

This traditional architecture is able to meet the functional requirements of its inhabitants. The thermal insulation and thermal storage properties of clay as a building material make it ideal for the dry savannah climate with ts considerable temperature

difference between day and night, extreme solar radiation from cloudless skies, the Harmattan wind and the cold winters.

The exemplary features of the architecture include: closed building forms with few openings, floor plans with protected internal spaces based on the 'reduit' principle of ecological architecture, sensible 'stacking' of functional areas – daytime spaces on the ground floor and night-time spaces on the upper floors that open onto roof terraces that can be used at night.

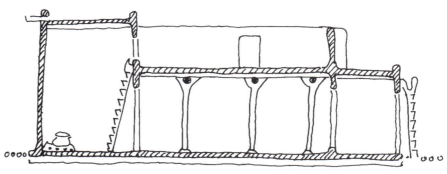

Plan and section showing a traditional two-storey dwelling house of the eastern plateau with its orthogonal/axial plan, and illustrating the 'reduit' principle in which the internal living area/hall and the external 'buffer spaces' are formed by the stores and the two-storey kitchen. The roof terrace between the bedrooms is sheltered from the wind.

Opposite page: The working area is located between the public space of the lane and the private spaces of the dwelling house. From the terrace it is easy to fill the uppermost grain store at attic level with dried heads of corn. The central 'reduit' space is lit by means of a roof light (left). A protective, mouth-like entrance leads from the forecourt to the small, central living room situated on the ground floor. The living room is a 'reduit' space climatically protected by the grain stores placed around it. On the upper level, the bedrooms are arranged around the central food store of the house.

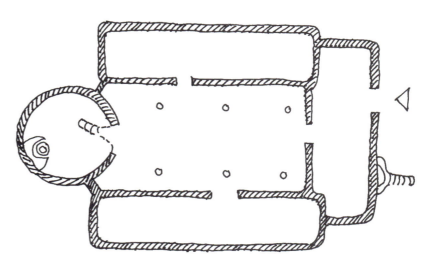

The dry, hot climatic zone of the savannah in northern Togo

Unlike the hot and humid climate of the coast, here the climate is determined by dryness, which is interrupted only during the short rainy season in summer by thunderstorms bringing heavy rainfall. The summer sun blazing from the cloudless skies of the high-pressure area at the northern tropic heats up the sparse vegetation of the savannah steppe to more than 40°C. By contrast, the winter months are extremely cold owing to the night-time radiation into the clear skies and the low level of ground moisture. Traditional architecture adapts to this extreme climate through the use of intelligent building forms, which are characterised by closed, solid clay construction with its good insulating and energy storage properties. In winter, the daytime warmth is stored and provides comfort in the internal living and bedrooms, whereas in summer the solid walls ensure the coolness of all the living spaces during the night.

The Tatas of the Tanberma are particularly impressive. These buildings, several storeys high, are built like defensive castles and are separated from their neighbours by the distance an arrow can fly. In this way the Tanberma peasants were able to defend themselves together during the time when they were hunted as prized slaves by the northern mounted tribes from what is today Burkina Faso.

The closed nature of the massive, external clay wall, with only a few ventilation openings and arrow slits which, at the same time, allow light to enter the dark interiors, represents an excellent climatic concept. The living room on the ground is climatically protected by the surrounding buffer spaces of the entrance area, the kitchen and the stables for small animals. The sleeping and storage area above also protects and insulates the living room-cum-hall below. The sleeping cells on the roof terrace are enclosed by a parapet and so offer a shielded area for women and children. As it lies on the elevated upper storey, this area is also cooled, even during the night, by the constant high-pressure wind from the north-east. The fact that the food stores are raised above the ground and 'guarded' by the sleeping areas arranged around them means that the stores containing peanuts, millet and maize are safe from thieves. The round forms made of the clay reinforced with limestone gravel – the settlement lies at the foot of a weathered range of limestone mountains – are structurally stiffened according to the principle of the eggshell, and are perfectly stable even though the walls are only between 15 and 18 centimetres thick.

In the West African savannah, with its wealth of intelligent architecture, anonymous builders developed the core house to a considerable level of sophistication.

The Lobi buildings in southern Burkina Faso demonstrate the principle of protected 'reduit' living spaces surrounded by insulating service spaces that are lit and ventilated from internal courtyards. Similar building types are found in the extreme climate of the rocky desert in Morocco's southern Atlas region with its hot summers and cold winters.

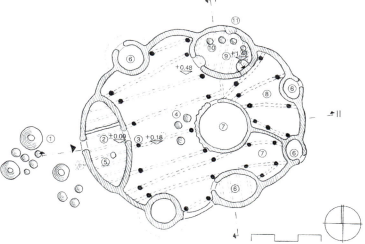

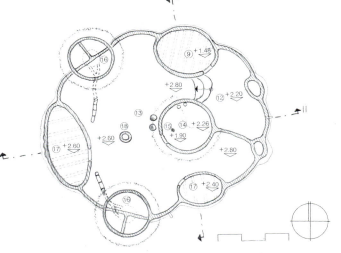

A dwelling of the Tanberma in northern Togo, with the entrance on the west side and fetishes placed in front of it

Ground-floor plan
1 Fetish
2 Entrance
3 Room
4 Fetish
5 Gully
6 Chicken coop
7 Stable
8 Sheep pen
9 Kitchen
10 Cooking hearth
11 Exhaust vent

Upper-floor plan
9 Kitchen
12 Mezzanine level
13 Roof level
14 Sleeping area for women and children
15 Gully
16 Grain store
17 Storeroom
18 Spyhole

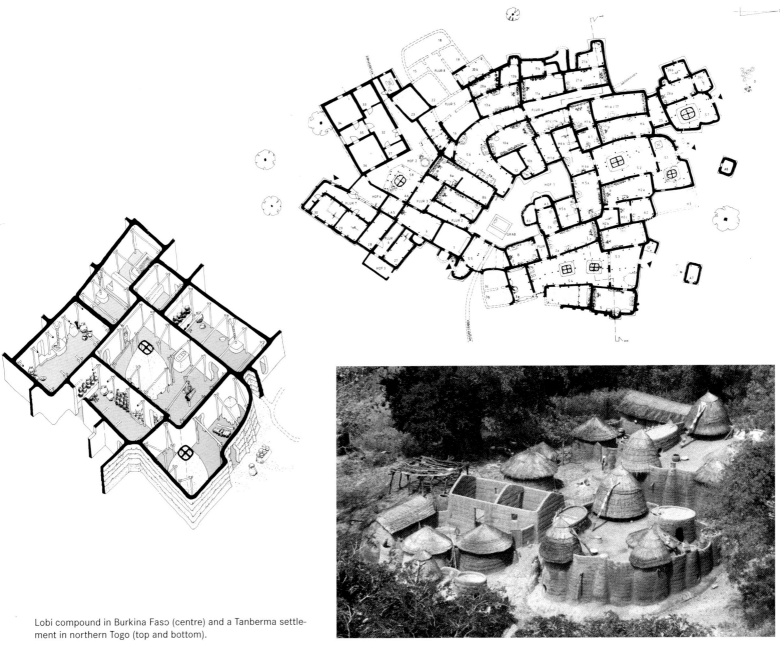

Lobi compound in Burkina Faso (centre) and a Tanberma settlement in northern Togo (top and bottom).

Entrance and roof terrace of a traditional settlement with animistic fetishes (above)

Section showing roof terrace, sleeping cells and protected grain store:
1 Entrance
2 Living area
3 Kitchen
4 Small domestic animals
5 Storeroom
6 Grain store
7 Sleeping cell

In his famous book *The Voice of Africa*, Leo Frobenius described the historic cave dwellings near Mopti, in Mali, which also have a central living cave surrounded by buffer spaces.

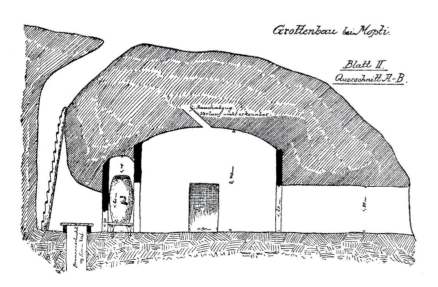

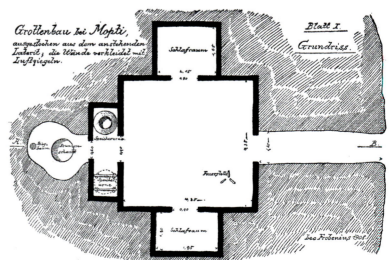

The traditional building form of the urban courtyard house in the savannahs of Africa and Asia

With the development of the town as a settlement type in the savannah of the Mesopotamian cultural area in the 4th millennium BC, the architectural problem arose of how to accommodate as many people as possible in the limited space of the walled town. The aim was to preserve an appropriate private sphere distinct from public urban space while enjoying the advantages offered by the town as a new, communicative living area for an urban society made up of traders, craftspeople and the new upper class of priests and rulers. The courtyard house type was developed as a solution to this problem. Through the internal courtyard the private living rooms could be lit and ventilated from within and the external walls could remain closed on three sides, making it possible to place the house close to the neighbouring buildings. Only through the entrance (and frequently via a small observation window) did the street side of the house open discreetly onto the street space. This is the most important advantage offered by the courtyard house: the separation of a private realm from the public nature of the busy street while using a relatively small site area.

This increase in density of the urban mesh is clearly recognisable in the early archaeological urban plan images from the third millennium of the Mesopotamian cultural area. In the still existing old towns of North Africa (Marrakesh) to the countries of the Near and Middle East, aerial photographs show the enormous density of urban space and the spaciousness of the private internal courtyards. Even in China this house type has stood the test of time over thousands of years in the large traditional towns.

A climatic advantage of the courtyard type house was – given the correct orientation of the access road or street in an east-west direction – that the main sides of the internal courtyard faced north or south. This made it easy to shade them against the sun when it was high in the sky by means of continuous verandas, as seen in the 'Moroccan house type' on page 77.

To improve their ventilation and shade, of the internal courtyards were surrounded by buildings two to three storeys high and were narrower in the north-south direction, which meant that large areas of the courtyard and the living rooms at ground-floor level

The old town of Djenné (above) in the River Niger now stands under UNESCO protection.

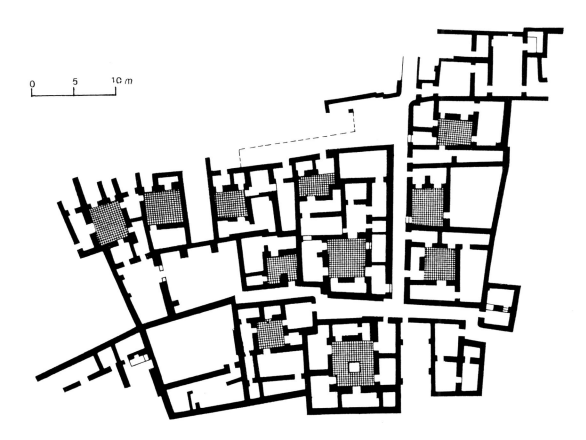

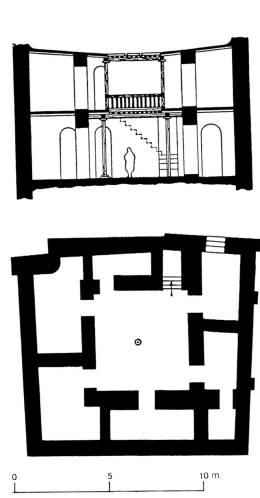

Examples of courtyard
houses in Djenné, Mali,
throughout 5,000 years
of human habitation.

were shaded by the surrounding access veranda,
while on the short east and west sides with the
sleeping quarters on the upper floor, the walls of the
internal courtyard were only minimally heated up by
the morning and evening sun, which stood at a lower
angle in the sky.

The tall cross-section of the internal courtyard functioned as a chimney for warm air rising during the
day. Cool air from the narrow lane that was still in
shadow in the morning could enter the courtyard
through the entrance doorway on the ground floor.
In addition, trees and fountains improved the micro-
climatic conditions in the private living areas by providing shade and through the coolness caused by
evaporation during the day, creating pleasant temperatures in the living and working spaces on the
ground floor, while the bedrooms on the upper level
were able to cool down by the evening. On balmy
summer evenings the roof terrace could also be
used as a pleasant outdoor sleeping area 'under a
thousand stars'. The courtyard-type house has
proved its worth for more than 5,000 years, as is
still confirmed today by the intact, pulsating inner
cities in Africa and the Orient, as far as China.

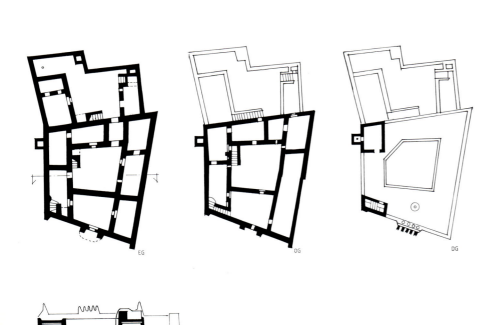

Djenné on the River Niger is one of the oldest towns in West Africa, founded after the first Islamic conquest by the Moroccan Almoravids in the 9th century AD.

The urban and architectural models from the northern Moroccan cultural area are recognisable in the layout of the town – with its narrow shaded lanes in which the typical North African multi-storey town courtyard houses lie – and also in the uniform clay architecture. The famous large mosque was erected at the end of the nineteenth century on old foundations and with its impressive façade determines the character of the market square.

Opposite page: the old market square in Djenné (top) and the narrow lanes and shaded courtyards of town dwellers' houses (bottom)

The living rooms face onto the deep, east-west oriented and shaded courtyards. The upper floor is reached by stairs and an internal, chain-like sequence of spaces or, in the case of square buildings, via a continuous veranda that provides shade for the courtyard façades (above).

The square Moroccan house type (right, after Swets, 1973):
1 L-shaped entrance screens the interior
2 Courtyard with fountain and tree
3 Living room
4 Salon
5 Kitchen
6 Bathroom
7 Guest room
8 Toilet

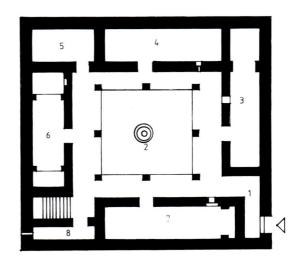

The old inner city of Fez in Morocco. The pulsating life in the shaded public lanes contrasts with the quiet of the private internal courtyards in which craftsmen work, *caravansereis* (hostels) are located, school lessons are given and family life goes on, often in a particularly introverted way, climatically protected by an accessible flat roof with a roof light (right).

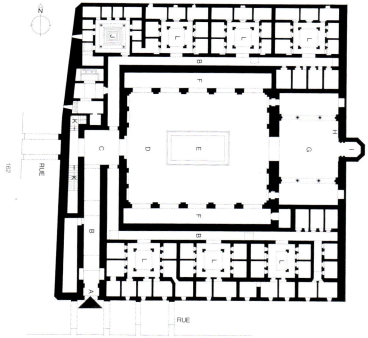

In the city of Marrakesh in southern Morocco this type of the simple courtyard house is found again in the large classic courtyard layout of the *medersa* of a notable, with protective small courtyards for the living and sleeping areas for staff and guests, the prayer room in the large internal courtyard, where water splashing in a fountain cools the space.

Typologies of traditional Chinese courtyard houses

The traditional Chinese courtyard-type house is an intelligent variation designed to suit the subtropical climate of China with its hot summers and often cool winter months. In contrast to the oriental courtyard house with its east-west orientation, closed west-east façades and the heavy shadow that results, the Chinese courtyard house is oriented north-south. This means that the east and west façades of the courtyard receive a good amount of sun in the morning and the evening.

The main buildings along a central axis are south-facing. In winter, they are warmed by the low south sun; in summer, deep verandas protect them from the summer sun that stands higher in the sky. The principle of the staggered entrance from the east-west oriented street to the private forecourt and main courtyards creates a highly intimate domestic quality. The fine, planted gardens that offer pleasant shade also make an important contribution to the quality of the living spaces.

Interestingly, this urban planning principle conforms with the early Egyptian example from the 2nd millennium (see page 66) of workers' settlements with courtyard houses along narrow roads running east-west.

Examples of traditional Chinese courtyard houses and interiors (above) and floor plans (right).

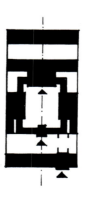

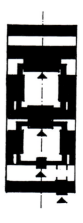

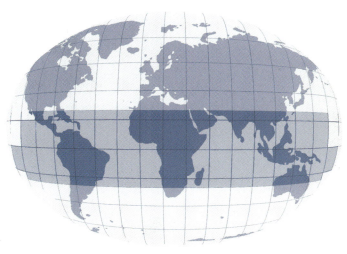

Fundamentals of Climatically Appropriate Building and Relevant Design Principles

A coffee plantation in the coastal mountains north of Rio de Janeiro with an open, well-ventilated terrace

A fisherman's dwelling on the banks of the Amazon River, Brazil

Some fundamentals of climatically appropriate design
Klaus Ferstl

The main concern of climatically appropriate design in architecture and urban planning is to create a building (or an urban structure) in such a way that an optimal (comfortable) or at least tolerable climate is created for the users, while employing as little energy and technical equipment as possible. At the same time, it must be ensured that the building construction itself suffers no damage from the climate (for example, damage caused by damp). The target function of climatically appropriate building is therefore always the indoor climate, whereby in our case, and in relation to housing, the following components are of primary importance:
thermal
  ► room air temperature
  ► surface temperature
hygric
  ► absolute humidity
  ► relative air humidity
air velocity in the immediate proximity of the users

The requirements made on each of these components are what ultimately decide whether and with what means and expenditure they can be maintained and stabilised at certain levels during the course of the day and throughout the year under the concrete conditions prevailing at each specific location.
The external climate, as well as the use to which the space is put, are 'disturbance variables' in terms of the indoor climate to be maintained. In a building that is neither heated nor cooled by technical means the components of the indoor climate in their diurnal (and annual) range follow the external ones. They are however amplitutude-modulated and phase-delayed. Again, the degree of that modification is determined mainly by:

  ► the flow of energy from outside due to solar radiation
  ► the flow of energy and emissions released by the use of the building
  ► the resistance of the building mantle to the transport of energy (thermal insulation)
  ► the heat storage capacity of the building's structure, as well as
  ► the airflow rate

The indoor climate can therefore also be purposefully influenced and determined by means of affecting these components, that is, by design decisions made in the following areas:
urban
  ► choice of the micro-location
  ► positioning of the building
  ► orientation of the building to the north
design
  ► floor plan solution
  ► size and arrangement of windows
  ► the type, construction and arrangement of shading devices
  ► shape of the roof
  ► choice of colour
building construction
  ► building method
  ► choice of materials
  ► building mass
  ► thermal insulation
  ► construction of the building parts and elements
as well as
utilization
  ► airflow rates/ventilation rates
  ► individual ventilation pattern of the users
  ► periods during which the building is used

Wherever, it is possible through considering and modifying these factors, to control the flow of energy and emissions and to harmonise them in such a way that the parameters envisaged for the indoor climate can be kept within given limits (at least during the period during which the building is in use), we talk of a building which is controlled by natural (structural) means.

However, where these natural or structural control mechanisms do not suffice or not entirely (for example, during extreme external conditions, or when, as is often the case in production buildings, for technological reasons high, precisely defined demands are made on the indoor climate), technical means (heating system, cooling system, humidifying or dehumidifying system) and, above all, (anthropogenous) energy provided specially for this purpose must be used to ensure that the parameters of the interior climate are achieved and kept within given limits. In such cases we talk of a mechanical climate control of the building.

Over the course of many centuries the extremely restricted technical and technological possibilities of creating energy available to man, which were almost exclusively based on wood as a source of energy, allowed no alternative to so-called natural climate control. Therefore the architectural design had to submit itself entirely, whether consciously or unconsciously, to these objective premises.[1] Characteristic of this epoch of development is a concept or architecture marked by regional differences and very much oriented to its immediate surroundings, because a direct relationship between the building and natural sources of energy, such as sun, wind or water, was an essential, indeed existential, necessity. Logically, wherever the source of energy available is still comparatively basic, for example, firewood, this relationship remains of primary importance.

A change of paradigm in the development of architecture first occurred towards the end of the 19th century, at least in the so-called industrialised countries. The basis for the supply of energy for society as a whole, as well as for individuals, changed dramatically: coal and, later, oil and natural gas now became relatively inexpensive sources of energy, and with the development of the major transport and energy distribution networks they were available at almost any desired location. Materials such as concrete, steel, glass and aluminium that now could be produced increasingly cheaply, replaced wood, natural stone and clay as the important building materials and thus altered the appearance of buildings and, indeed, of entire cities in a fundamental way. Electric motors and electric lighting allowed deeper and, above all, taller buildings and, not least significantly, on the basis of these new possibilities, rapidly developing heating, ventilation and air-conditioning technology tended increasingly to take on the functions of regulating the indoor climate, functions that had previously been undertaken almost entirely by the building and its design.

As a consequence the creation of the interior climate and the design of the building tended to go their separate ways. As early as 1922 Ludwig Mies van der Rohe showed the logical consequences of this development in his programmatic designs for high-rise buildings: free development of the architectural form, the building shell as a highly transparent or completely glazed skin and the transfer of the task of creating a suitable indoor climate (and with it, the guarantee of the function) to an accordingly efficient technical system.

This fundamental design concept of Modernism has, more or less, not only influenced the architecture of the highly developed industrialised countries to a greater or lesser degree, but, as the so-called 'International Style' and a symbol of economic productivity and power, has also exerted its influence on building activity in numerous tropical countries.

Recently-built hotels on the coast of Togo with an incorrect orientation towards the sun.

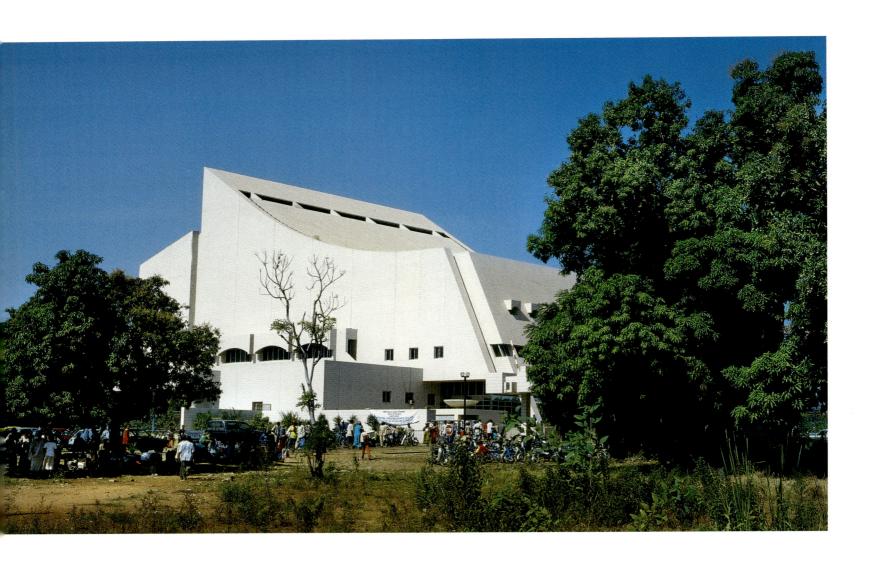

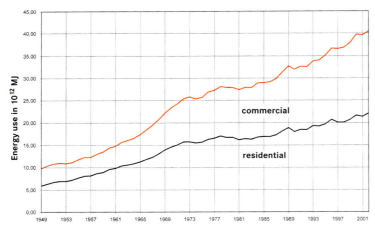

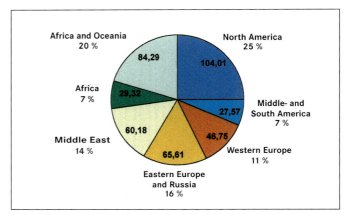

But what have been the consequences?
In the developed industrialised countries this architectural concept led as early as the middle of the previous century to an enormous increase in the consumption of energy in both the public and private sectors. In the majority of these countries, although they mostly lie in temperate climatic zone, this amount of energy is between 20 and 40 per cent of the total energy consumption. Of this energy consumption, on average three quarters is needed for the heating, cooling and lighting of buildings. In the USA alone between 1950 and 2000 energy consumption in the private and public sector increased more than fourfold and in 2000 it amounted to almost 40×10^{12} MJ (opposite page, bottom left). For most of those tropical countries that, for a number of different motives, followed this kind of architectural development, expenditure of this magnitude was and remains an illusion. On the one hand, because the amount of energy required for this kind of climate control is simply not available in these countries, while on the other hand, the energy actually available is, as a rule, far more urgently required for other purposes – for example, for the

economic development of the country, for production and trade –than to air-condition poorly designed housing and office buildings. For example, as shown on the previous page (bottom right), in 2000 the *primary* energy production of the entire continent of Africa amounted to 29×10^{12} MJ. This is not even three quarters of the amount of *final* energy that was 'consumed' in the same period in the private and public sectors in the USA alone.

Anyone who has often visited tropical countries knows the fate that generally befalls these glazed messengers of a dubious architectural trend: energy-intensive air-conditioning systems, if any have been installed in the first place, are turned on only in exceptional cases and on special occasions, or not at all. As the buildings themselves have almost no features that can regulate the climate, outside of these operating times the indoor climate rapidly becomes intolerable, which in turn limits the usefulness of the building, frequently making it impossible to use. Furthermore, the users of buildings run in this way are often exposed to serious health risks: as the air conditioning systems are, as a rule, only sporadically serviced and cleaned (if at all), they spread dirt particles, micro-organisms, bacteria and germs very quickly in the rooms to be air-conditioned or, indeed, throughout the entire building. But even a technogenously air-conditioned, i.e. mechanically-controlled, building requires that the design of the building be climatically appropriate and adapted to its particular location. Whereas, however, in the case of a building climatically controlled by natural means, the level of its adaptation to the climate of the site decides whether (or with what level of exception) the parameters of indoor climate can be maintained at all. In the case of mechanically controlled indoor climate this level of adoption determines the necessary technical effort, the expenditure of energy and, with it, the economic efficiency. Especially this economic aspect is of significance

A conference centre in Bamako (top)

Energy use in US residential and commercial sectors[2] (bottom left).
World primary energy production 2000[3] (in 10^{12} MJ) (bottom right)

above all for countries in the warm regions of the earth, as the 'removal' of a kilocalorie of energy for cooling purposes is between five and ten times more expensive than 'introducing' the same amount of energy for heating purposes. For this reason more than a few of the 'International Style' prestige objects erected in the Tropics today remain unused and stand as sad witnesses to a misguided investment policy, because their owners can no longer meet the costs of running these energy-devouring monsters.

But it is not solely economic criteria or, as is argued, the 'limited availability of energy' associated with the very real threat of exhausting our non-renewable energy sources that force us to fundamentally reconsider the idea of climatically appropriate design adapted to each particular location. Far more serious is the fact that, in most of the developed countries, a certain upper limit has already been reached in relation to the disposal and the safe degradation (for both man and his environment) of the constantly increasing amount of waste and rest-products resulting from the 'production' of energy. To this extent man today has not so much reached an 'energy branching point' but rather an 'upper disposal limit' that requires us to develop new, ecologically-based development concepts, also in the fields of architecture and urban planning. This applies not only to the developed industrial countries of Europe, America and Asia but (and above all) also to the numerous developing and newly industrialising countries in tropical regions. In the past few years building climatology and building physics have supplied an important theoretical foundation. On the basis of a mathematical model of the interdependency between the external climate, the building and the indoor climate, there now exists a truly comprehensive system of methods with the aid of which the indoor climate of a building (or at least its most important

parameters) can be precalculated, and its temporal progression simulated already during the planning process. Simulation calculations of this kind not only demand complex (and therefore generally expensive) computer technology (both hard and software) but also, and most importantly, they require truly comprehensive and correct data material. Besides specific data on physical and structural properties of the utilised building materials, this data includes, first of all, the specification of the climate of each particular site. And, in most cases this site is not identical with the location of the meteorological station. Whereas in countries with a relatively dense network of meteorological stations the imprecision of computer calculations resulting from such local differences can still be compensated without a noteworthy diminution of the reliability of the calculated result, in the case of tropical countries that often have only a few such meteorological stations (generally in the capital and a small number of larger cities), these inaccuracies are too great to be balanced out, even with the use of sophisticated and efficient computing technology. In those cases, the dominance of local climatic influences, when compared with the macroclimatic influences, is simply too great. In addition, there is the fact that meteorological stations generally evaluate the data they record mainly from the viewpoint of agriculture, that is, in terms of growth criteria and vegetation and less in terms of those values that are of interest for technogenous processes (for example, mean daytime temperatures in the warmest and the coldest months, coldest and warmest pentates, dew point temperatures, etc.). Therefore, in their work in the Tropics, planners can, and indeed must, rely primarily on two sources of information:

- ► easy-to-use methods for preliminary calculations of building climate that require only a relatively limited supply of data

► a goal-oriented analysis of those design elements in autochthonous buildings that modify the interior climate and the construction principles that can be derived from them to form a generally valid design canon

Autochthonous or traditional buildings are those that have crystallised (generally over a longer period of time) under the specific social, cultural, technical, technological and, above all, climatic circumstances prevailing in a certain region. In terms of building climatology, the most interesting are those built solutions in which the function has changed little in the course of time or which have survived largely in their original form. These are, primarily, traditional forms of housing and the settlement structures in which they are found. As the numerous examples shown in this book confirm, this is also where one finds the most striking and impressive examples of an architecture that, in the truest sense of the phrase, is designed in a climatically appropriate and responsive way.

Similar climatic conditions produce a similar basic model (a so-called archetype) for buildings and settlement patterns, albeit with a range of different forms. Massive and compact buildings made from relatively heavy building materials and arranged in a dense and closed settlement pattern are to be found in the hot and dry climatic zone; in warm and humid climates, the prevailing form is the lightweight building, generally elevated above the ground, allowing the passage of air and wind, and organised in a scattered, more open settlement. Departing from this 'archetype', as our ancestors knew well, always meant having either to accept the use of increased energy (and therefore economic) expenditure – presuming, of course, that stability and an appropriate lifespan could be ensured in the first place – or to understand the building primarily as a demonstration or representative display piece, free of any prag-

matic function and therefore not subject to stringent requirements in terms of interior climate.

How might we employ these traditional design criteria to create buildings which, given the rapid growth in population, must be suited for industrial mass production, that is, must be made under completely different technical and technological circumstances and that, above all, must take into account entirely new social aspirations?

It is certain that the answer to this question differs greatly from place to place and is dependant on a number of very different factors. It must also lead in each case to locally different and regionally specific solutions. The answer most definitely does not lie in the mere formal application of external design elements, which, though they may increase the decorative effect of modern buildings, do not inevitably have the effect on the interior building climate that they possibly had in their traditional 'parent house'. And it is equally certain that an answer cannot be based on a high-tech concept that requires far too much energy for most tropical countries, or on a socially indefensible 'back to nature' movement that in any case is generally perceived in these countries as discriminatory.

In my opinion, the only sensible approach to a solution lies in analysing the principles of traditional autochthonous building (in as far as they have an effect on the interior climate) on the basis of sound knowledge about building climatology, and processing them to define generally valid and recognised rules of building, while also, through the training and further education of planners, builders and clients, providing a basis for both the design and development of new, up-to-date housing forms and building technologies, as well as for the establishment of appropriate user behaviour patterns. Some of these basic design principles are examined below.

What demands are to be made on the indoor climate?

The decisive factor in the requirements made on the indoor climate is the user of the internal space and therefore the behaviour of the human organism in terms of heat physiology is of particular importance. For the preservation of all normal bodily functions a more or less constant deep body temperature of 37°C ± 0,5 K is necessary. The thermal energy required for this is produced by exothermal reaction, that is, by the 'burning' of food supplied to the body. Surplus heat (in an adult human this is a daily average of about 80 W) is released to the environment through the skin (90 per cent) and the breath (around 10 per cent). When a person carries out work, this so-called basic energy conversion is increased by the amount of the work energy conversion. Depending on the kind of work performed, this lies at about a factor of 3 times the basic energy conversion rate. In the case of extremely heavy manual labour for short periods (5 to 10 minutes), the factor can be as high as 20 times the basic energy conversion rate.

At an ambient temperature of around 20°C, about 80 per cent of the heat produced by the body is transported to the surroundings in a 'dry' manner, that is by convection, radiation and (to a small extent) also by thermal conduction, and about 20 per cent in a 'wet' manner, namely, by the evaporation of moisture.[4] If the ambient temperature increases, the proportion of dry heat emission decreases and the amount of wet heat emission increases (and with it the amount of water vapour emitted). In addition, the body is thermally relieved by the cooling effect of evaporation.

If this energy conversion is not prevented the body finds itself in a thermal balance with its surroundings. The heat balance is then regulated by 'latent physical heat regulation', that is, by the autonomous nervous system alone.[5] This kind of interior climate is described as 'optimal (comfortable)' and is not consciously perceived at all by the vegetative nervous system, that is, by human sense.

The sensible regulation of heat, which is controlled by the vegetative nervous system and therefore consciously registered by humans, first takes over when the climate differs from the optimal values. This kind of difference is always associated with a reduction in the feeling of well-being and ultimately also with a decline in the productive efficiency of human beings. This is permissible (and, as will be shown later, is almost unavoidable in the Tropics) as long as the health of human beings is not seriously affected or endangered. This type of climate is therefore also described as 'acceptable' or 'tolerable'.

Optimal conditions:
Where there is only slight air movement, that is to say, at air velocities of up to 0.3 m/s, the optimal values for room temperature lie between 22 and 26°C (opposite page, top left). Temperatures of up to 29°C are still perceived as comfortable if the air movement also increases, whereby air velocities above 0.8 m/s are no longer experienced as comfortable. In an optimal climate humidity has only a slight influence and can range between 20 and 90 per cent. Values below 30 per cent should, however, be avoided to prevent excessive drying of the mucous membranes; with values over 80 per cent there is a danger of falling below the dew point and with it the associated danger of damage to the building construction caused by condensation.

Tolerable conditions:
In the case of almost still air in warm climatic zones, temperatures of up to around 30°C can be regarded as tolerable (opposite page, top centre). In such a case (and in contrast to the optimum climate), air humidity, in addition to air movement, also has a

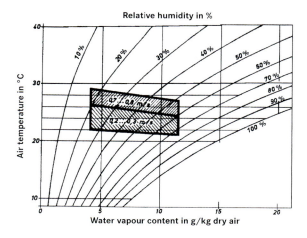

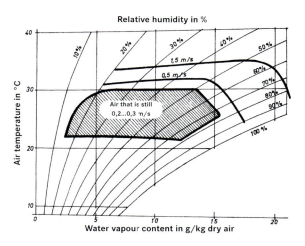

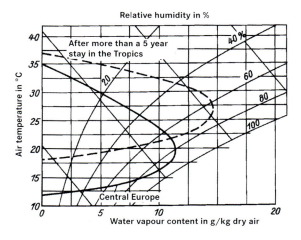

'Cosiness' inside a traditional mud structure (top right)

Optimal (comfortable) climate conditions (valid for a gross energy conversion of 60–70 W/m² – i.e. office work – and a thermal resistance of clothing of 0.3–0.6 clo - i.e. light khaki)[10] (top)

Range of tolerable climate conditions after acclimatisation to warm climates depending on diverse wind conditions[10] (centre)

Shifting of tolerable climatic conditions in case of a prolonged stay in the Tropics, compared with the temperate climate of Central Europe[8] (bottom)

significant influence on our sensitivity to the interior climate. Above the mugginess level, which lies at a water vapour content of about 15 g/kg, a climate is tolerable only with an air velocity of over 0.5 m/s. An air velocity of 1.5 m/s is generally regarded as the upper tolerable limit.

As Fanger[7] already noted in 1970, human sensitivity to climate is, at least in the optimal range, independent of climatic zone and race. Thanks to its ability to emit additional heat by sweating the human organism is able to adapt from a temperate to a warm climate within a few days or weeks. By contrast, the range experienced as tolerable adjusts, as the illustration bottom left shows, to the climatic conditions in the Tropics only over a longer period of time (5 to 7 years). This must be taken into account, for example when planning accommodation for persons who will spend only a relatively short time in the Tropics.

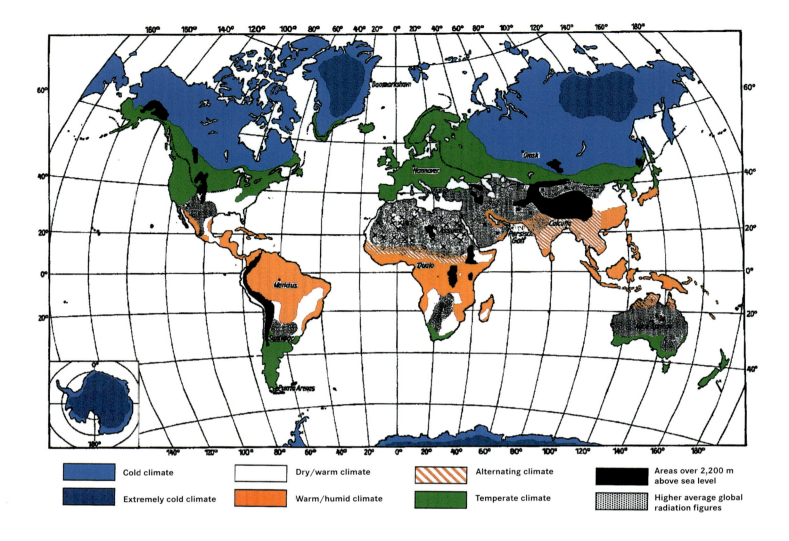

■	Cold climate	□	Dry/warm climate	▨	Alternating climate	■ Areas over 2,200 m above sea level
■	Extremely cold climate	■	Warm/humid climate	■	Temperate climate	▦ Higher average global radiation figures

Some fundamental principles of climatically appropriate building in the warm and dry climatic zone

Characteristics of the climatic zone

For the concerns of climatically appropriate building, the most useful is the mapping of the world into climatic zones from a technical viewpoint, as suggested by Böer in 1964.[9] Böer distinguishes between 5 main climate zones:

► the cold climate
► the temperate climate
► the warm and dry climate
► the warm and humid climate and
► the alternating climate

In the tropical regions, that is, in the area extending between the Tropic of Cancer (23°26' latitude north of the equator) and the Tropic of Capricorn (23°26' south of the equator), the climatic zones encountered are warm climates and the alternating climate (see the overview map above). Regions with an extremely

warm climate are marked with an X on the map. According to Böer, those climatic regions can be regarded as warm and dry in which at least in one month the normal value of the mean monthly temperature lies above 22°C, without the simultaneous occurrence of high monthly mean relative humidity values (opposite page, top). The daily temperature amplitude can show values of between 10 and 15 K (opposite page, bottom). As a result, on the one hand, the air temperatures can be extremely high (the normal value of the annual maximum lies at around 45°C, extreme temperatures even reach levels of between 50 and 55°C), while on the other hand, temperatures around freezing point are not unusual. The minimum mean daily temperature in the coldest month is around -14°C, the normal value of the annual minimum is around -15°C. High global radiation (in extreme cases up to 980 W/m^2) is characteristic of hot and dry climates, as are considerable amounts of sand and dust in the air.

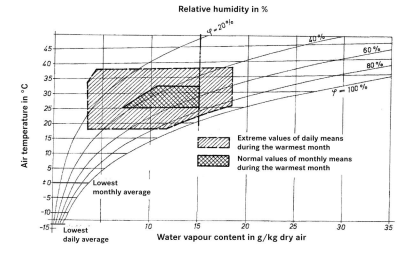

Relative humidity in %

Extreme values of daily means during the warmest month

Normal values of monthly means during the warmest month

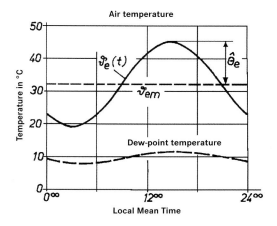

Design criteria

In a warm and dry climate, protection against solar radiation and the associated high air temperatures plays the dominant role. The heat-retaining capacity of the buildings, which describes the hygro-thermal behaviour of the construction and links the heat storage capacity with the airflow rate, must be as great as possible. To achieve this level of heat-retaining capacity a building must have high to very high heat-storage capacity and, at least during the hot periods of the day, should be only minimally ventilated or not at all.

Therefore, compact and massive buildings, whose walls, ceilings and floors are made of relatively heavy materials, are typical of warm and dry regions. Traditional buildings were generally built of clay and natural stone. Today these have been largely replaced by concrete blocks and fired bricks, although both the production and transport of such materials are relatively energy-intensive.

The bulk density of the materials used should, where possible, not be less than 1,500 kg/m³. To ensure an adequate storage capacity, the constructional thickness of massive exterior walls (thermally stressed on one side) should be at least 8 to 10 cm and of massive internal walls (thermally stressed on both sides) at least 16 to 20 cm. In addition, floor plans with a number of small parts and a high proportion of interior walls – and therefore a very large area of interior wall surface to store heat – increase the storage capacity of a building. Characteristic of hot regions is, for example, the widespread use of niches along the inner wall surfaces and a stalactite-like treatment of the room corners.

As a rule the buildings are not elevated above ground and generally do not have a basement, which allows the storage effect of the ground to be exploited. Where, in addition to the diurnal changes, there are considerable fluctuations in the outside temperature during the course of the year – for example, in the desert areas of the central and southern Sahara – we often encounter underground and cave dwellings. However, where the differences between the seasonal temperatures are more moderate – for example, close to the coast or near large lakes – the moderating effect exerted by surfaces in contact with the ground on the amplitude of the indoor air temperature is relatively slight. Therefore, in such regions we encounter not only lighter but frequently also taller buildings, up to several storeys high, which are detached from the heat-storage properties of the ground and which

Classification of the world's climate according to BÖER[9] (opposite page)

Extreme values of daily means and normal values of monthly means during the hottest and the coldest month in warm-dry climates[9] (top)

Typical daily course of outdoor air temperature and dew-point temperature in warm-dry climates[10] (bottom)

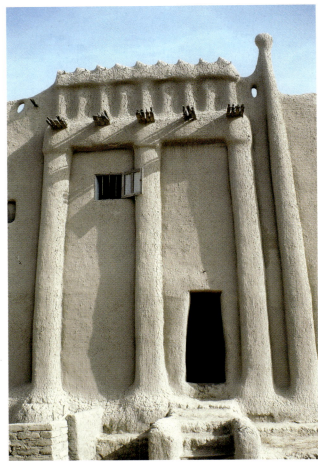

Opposite page: examples of
traditional clay architecture
in the African savannah region

prefer to expose their exterior surfaces to the cooling breezes that come generally from the sea. Effective shading of the entire building shell is of major importance for thermal protection. In traditional architecture the shading of the exterior walls is first of all achieved by a closed and very dense settlement pattern. Only narrow lanes were arranged between the individual buildings (which, for wind protection, were generally all the same height) so that the buildings shaded each other from the sun. An inner courtyard enclosed on all sides by living and service rooms or by walls functioned as a private outdoor area in which family life was conducted during the day. This inner courtyard was shaded either by plants, where the vegetation allowed this, or by partial or complete roofing. In the houses of the well-off there were often water basins, small fountains or stones over which water trickled in these courtyards and in the living rooms opening onto them. Thanks to the physical effect of evaporative cooling, these features ensured an effective reduction of the air temperature.

The narrow lanes in traditional developments, were angled and staggered in relation to each other so that the (generally hot) wind could not blow unhindered through them and the settlement could also be made 'windproof' to the outside with relative ease.

Through their positioning alone these external walls were protected from the sun and the wind and could therefore be relatively thin, whereas in the case of a free-standing building, adequate thermal protection required the use of very thick walls, that is, considerable material expenditure. Therefore, in such cases, efforts were first made to provide help through the use of trees and shrubs (local vegetation growth permitting) or with the help of movable shading systems (woven screens or mats made of leaves

or grass) that could be placed as required against the exterior walls. These elements also provided protection against sand and dust storms.

In traditional houses of the warm and dry zone, windows were generally not found at all or, where essential, were very small and could be shaded completely throughout the day by screens or awnings. Thus only the roof was directly exposed to the sun and this element was therefore traditionally made of heavy materials with good thermal insulating properties. In addition, the area of roof was kept as small as possible, for instance, by the use of upward tapering building forms. The exterior surfaces of the roof were, in addition, always very bright (as indeed were the exterior walls), to absorb as little radiation as possible and to keep their surface temperature low. As the roofs generally served as a sleeping area at night they were shaded from the sun during the day with sails made of cloth or mats of leaves or grass and were thus protected from overheating. In a sense, constructions of this kind represent the primal form of a two-skin ventilated roof.

The means of ventilating the building itself had to be extremely flexible: during the day, to optimise the storage capacity of the heavy structure, only very little (hot) outside air could be allowed to flow through the building. The openings (which in any case were kept as small as possible) were thus generally kept closed. However, during the night, when the outside air had already cooled down, it was essential to be able to ventilate with a considerable airflow in order to 'discharge' the storage mass of the building and cool it down. If the wind alone did not suffice to provide this level of ventilation, rooftop elements or, as in several areas on the Persian Gulf, special wind towers were used to provide chimney-type ventilation shafts that worked through thermal buoyancy alone.

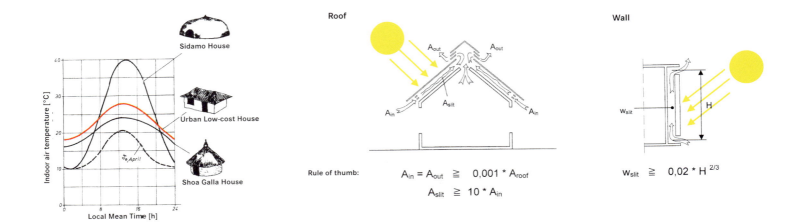

Sidamo House

Urban Low-cost House

Shoa Galla House

Indoor air temperature [°C]

$\vartheta_{e, April}$

Local Mean Time [h]

Roof

A_{out} A_{out}

A_{slit}

A_{in} A_{in}

Wall

W_{slit} H

Rule of thumb: $A_{in} = A_{out} \geqq 0,001 * A_{roof}$

$A_{slit} \geqq 10 * A_{in}$

$W_{slit} \geqq 0,02 * H^{2/3}$

Nowadays the forms of settlement in tropical countries are also increasingly determined by motorised traffic. The old, narrow lanes that provided welcome shade have had to yield to broad streets that offer the sun and the hot winds plenty of space. This has decisive consequences for the design of buildings, as the thermal protection of the exterior walls and roofs must be ensured either by means of efficiently back-ventilated shade systems mounted on the outside of the building or, alternatively, by an additional layer of thermal insulation (a simple calculation system is shown, for example, in the publication by Petzold and Hoinka[11]). Compact buildings are here more suitable than a fragmented volume with an extensive façade. The main façade of the building should always face between south-east and south-west (north of the equator) or north-east and north-west (south of the equator) as, at the time of maximum radiation, the sun is very high in the sky and effective shade can be provided by simple fixed horizontal screens or louvres. On the east and west façades maximum radiation occurs when the sun is relatively low in the sky. Here, effective shade is possible only with the use of flexible sunshade systems, which are generally not only more expensive but, above all, more fault-prone and thus often do not work for very long.

As the previous examples show, the thermally effective heavy roof construction of the traditional houses is increasingly being replaced by thin and extremely light constructions, for example, single layers of corrugated metal. However, even if they have an extremely light-coloured external surface, such constructions heat up considerably in comparison with the thick, heavy grass and clay roofs with their effective insulating properties. Owing to their low mass these modern roofs transport the peak temperatures (temperatures of between 100 and 120°C can occur for short periods) almost immediately to the interior surface of the building. In summer these metal roofs then function as a kind of ceiling-mounted radiant heating system for an interior which is in any case already very warm!

Within a society that still functions according to traditional rites and has a village structure in which daytime life is generally led outdoors, this may have no serious consequences for the practical use of buildings, because when this 'radiant heating' system is operating, as a number of examples from Ethiopia (illustrated above left) make clear, the air temperatures inside are also high, but in traditional houses nobody uses these rooms at this time of the day. For a house in a town, however, where there is no private outdoor space and therefore family life during the daytime must take place inside the building, this kind of construction is clearly completely unsuitable. Lightweight roof structures (and the roof slabs made of burnt-clay and concrete tiles now widely used in the Tropics are included in this category) should be used in warm and dry areas with high solar radiation intensity only as part of a double-layer construction, that is, in conjunction with an inner shell that is as heavy as possible and very well insulated. The clear width between the inner and outer shell is necessary to ensure intensive ventilation and thus to conduct the radiant warmth from the lightweight upper layer directly to the outside as rapidly as possible (above right). As the illustration also shows, a ventilated exterior wall can function in an analogous fashion. Where, due to the frequency of sand or dust storms, or for other reasons, this kind of ventilation of the building shell is not feasible, lightweight constructions should not be used.

Calculated mean indoor air temperatures of different traditional houses (opposite page, left) of the Central Ethiopian Highlands (on a sunny day in April, i.e. before the rainy season) [12]

Designing rules for ventilated double-layer (clam-shell) structural members (opposite page, right)

Courtyard of the Alhambra (below) in Granada, with shading of the loggias and cooling by fountains

The changes in lifestyles and the increasing movement of life from the traditional outdoor space to the interior of a building have further consequences for building design in the warm and dry climatic zone. First, there is the inevitable demand for better lighting of the interiors, and, in turn, for more and larger windows. Even with the use of effective shade systems, this raises the external thermal load very considerably when compared with traditional buildings. Secondly, the interior thermal load is also considerably higher than in traditional buildings because people spend more time indoors and also because of the numerous technical appliances that are nowadays a standard part of a modern household. Thirdly, on this account, the airflow rate during the day must be increased, which in turn means that the heat-retaining capacity of modern housing is always less than in a traditional building, even in structures with the same effective thermal storage building mass. Fourthly and lastly, owing to the extension of the period during which the building is used, an acute demand has arisen which requires that the internal climate parameters defining human comfort also be maintained during the day, that is, during the period of maximum thermal stress from the exterior climate, and no longer only during the night (when the thermal load reduces), as was generally the case in traditional housing.

Modern housing must therefore apply the basic principles of climatically appropriate design in a far more principled and rigorous way than was ever the case in traditional architecture.

Main principles of climatically appropriate building in the warm and dry climatic zone

Settlement and urban structure

These include a dense, closed development and a 'winding' layout of narrow lanes and streets to combat the hot, sand-carrying winds (trade winds). Walls or dense, protective planting form wind barriers at the edge of the settlements. The tall buildings on either side of the narrow streets shade each other. Trees with broad crowns offer shade on the streets, in squares and courtyards, and additional shade is provided by translucent awnings made of light material, and by mesh screens or pergolas with climbing plants.

Building typology

This involves a closed architecture with internal core zones (reduit) or internal courtyards, as well as compact multi-storey buildings in closely placed groups, and terrace houses or courtyard houses with verandas and tall, shaded courtyards. The main building is closed to the outside and opens only onto shaded veranda passageways or tall internal courtyards ventilated by a chimney effect (thermal buoyancy). Additional improvement to the microclimate is achieved through fountains and planting in the courtyard. Flat roofs (owing to low rainfall) are well shaded during the day and can be used as sleeping terraces in the cooler nights.

The effects of solar radiation are reduced by:
- north-south orientation of the main building façades. Buildings are closed to the east and west to protect them against the low morning and evening sun.
- internal core zones (bedrooms) protected by an external ring of buffer spaces.
- the time of the day during which the rooms in the building are used, as this determines their position within the building, namely

bedrooms on the east-south-east side release the heat stored during the day in the early hours of the evening, whereas living rooms and work areas on the west-north-west side release their heat in the later hours of the evening when people are asleep (early sunset in the tropics)

Building design and construction

The emphasis here is on massive construction using heavy, energy-storing materials – such as a single layer of clay or natural stone and concrete with an inner, double-layer shell providing thermal insulation – and on closed building volumes with only a few openings for light and ventilation.

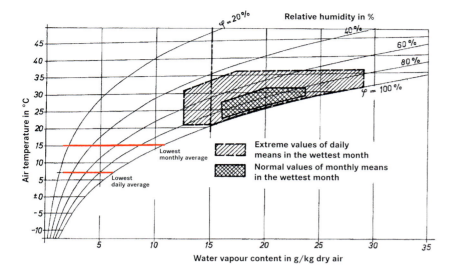

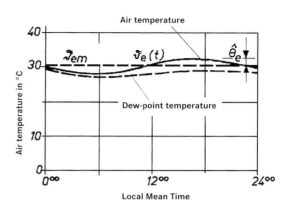

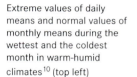

Extreme values of daily means and normal values of monthly means during the wettest and the coldest month in warm-humid climates[10] (top left)

Typical daily course of outdoor air temperature and dew-point temperature in warm-humid climates[10] (top right)

Some fundamental principles of climatically appropriate building in the warm and humid climatic zone

Characteristics of the climatic zone

In the warm and humid climatic zone the intensity of solar radiation is lower than in the warm and dry zone. A large proportion of the radiated solar energy is fixed as latent heat through evaporation, so that air temperatures do not rise to the extremes of the warm and dry climatic zone. However, the water vapour content of the air is considerably greater and it is muggy practically all the time. According to Böer, climatic regions can be classed as warm and humid where, in at least one month, the normal mean monthly temperature lies above 20°C and, in addition, the normal value of the relative humidity in this month exceeds 80 per cent (above). The normal total monthly precipitation often exceeds 200 mm. Heavy rainfall, during which considerable amounts of precipitation fall within a short period, often in association with hurricane-like storms, is typical of warm and humid climate zones.

In contrast to the warm and dry climate, air temperatures vary little, either during the day or throughout the year (above right).

Regions in which certain seasons occur regularly each year, of which one, viewed in isolation, can be described as a warm and humid season and the others as dry and warm, are described by Böer as regions with an 'alternating climate'. This climatic zone, which is indicated by diagonal hatching in the overview map on page 94 , should, from the viewpoint of climatically appropriate design, be treated as a warm and humid climate. Because of the warm and dry period of the year, tolerable indoor climatic conditions can be created in an alternating climate by means of adequate air movement, just like in a warm and humid climate. By contrast, if the kind of massive construction suited to warm and dry climates were used, it would be impossible to avoid damage by condensation during the warm and humid period of the year

Design criteria

For human beings the sultry climate of the warm and humid zone is the most difficult and is acceptable only if there is sufficient air movement. Optimal climatic conditions, can therefore only be ensured through the use of forced air-conditioning, that is, by means of cooling and dehumidifying the air coming from outside – an energy-intensive and expensive operation. However, with correct climatically adjusted design it is nevertheless possible to achieve a tolerable room climate in warm and humid climates using only natural climate control, as many traditional buildings show. The primary design rule is always to ensure sufficient air movement in the living areas. As the illustration on page 95 clearly shows, in the warmest months air velocities of between 1 and 1.5 m/s are necessary. At the same time, the living areas must be screened from any additional thermal load (caused, for example, by solar radiation) and also from any additional water vapour load (caused, for example, by cooking or washing).

The basis for adequate ventilation of living areas should already be provided by the urban planning design. The architect must therefore inform himself about the prevailing wind and airflow conditions in the area. Locations exposed to the wind, such as

Airflow around a building (left)

Spacing of buildings in warm-humid climates (right)

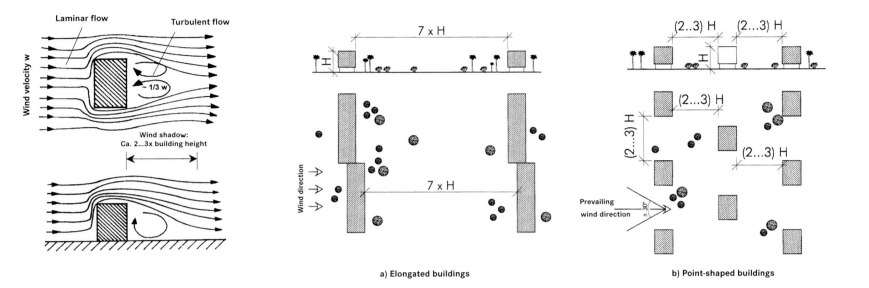

a) Elongated buildings   b) Point-shaped buildings

mountain ridges, mountain slopes, the shores of large lakes or the coastline, have always been and still remain preferable for housing in these regions. The streets and open spaces should be laid out in the direction of the prevailing winds, and the buildings, where possible, placed with their main façade in a transverse direction (±30°). With a divergence of 45° to the main wind direction the pressure of the incident wind flowing against the façade is reduced by about 50 per cent. In the flow direction, as shown above, a wind-shadow is formed behind the building with an air current that is predominantly turbulent but reduced to only about three quarters of its original velocity. The length of this wind-shadow, also known as the 'dead water area', is in the case of narrow, approximately point-shaped buildings around two to three times the building height, but in the case of elongated buildings can be up to seven times the building height. Therefore, to ensure an even (laminar) flow along the main façades, in warm and humid regions the distance between the buildings must be as large as possible (in contrast to the situation in hot and dry climates), and of such a size that the building is completely outside the wind-shadow of neighbouring buildings (above right). If only because of the restricted area of land usually available within a city, a development of tall, approximately point-shaped buildings arranged in a chequerboard pattern is preferable to a development consisting of elongated, closed rows of buildings.

According to the nature of the terrain, the wind speed increases with the height above the earth's surface (opposite page, left). Rooms lying at greater heights are therefore better exposed to the wind than those directly at ground level, especially as the latter are often screened from the wind by trees, shrubs and plants. Therefore, elevated houses with high roofs and deep overhangs (because of heavy rainfall) that protect the walls against both the rain and the sun are characteristic of traditional development in many regions of the warm and humid zone. Raising the building is also advantageous as it reduces its heat-retaining capacity and also avoids the problem of rising damp from the ground. Moreover, such 'stilt houses' are much better protected against high tides and floods than houses on ground level.

Wind velocity gradients (below left)

Schematic floor plan of a dwelling house adapted to
warm-humid climates (right)

Measurement rules for cross ventilation (below right)

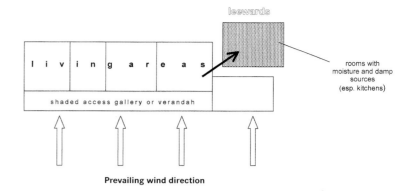

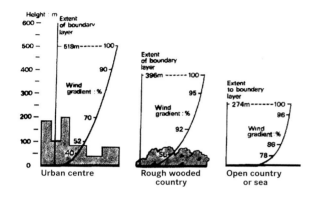

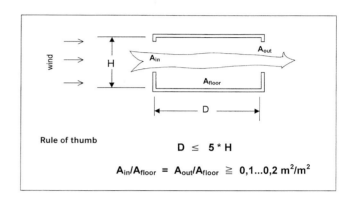

Because of the need for solar protection, the long sides of a building, as in the warm and dry climatic zone, should generally be oriented to the south and to the north in both hemispheres. If this orientation is not the same as the prevailing wind direction, the dominant wind conditions are decisive for the orientation of the main façade (in contrast to the situation in the warm and dry zone). However, in such cases, full shade must be provided which can considerably raise the investment and maintenance costs of the shading systems.

Both the floor plan and the geometry of the space must allow the cross-ventilation of the living areas. The schematic floor plan in (top right) – in which the living rooms are arranged in a row beside one another and are accessed from an open veranda or gallery that at the same time functions as effective solar protection – is ideal. Groups of spaces with considerable heat or moisture loads should be separated from the living areas and arranged on the leeside of the building so that the heat and moisture loads can be dissipated directly to the outside to avoid additional stress on the living areas (see page 107). According to Petzold,[10] the airflow rate required for housing is 100 to 200 m³ per m² ground area or gross floor area. This is on average a 50-fold air exchange. To achieve this with natural ventilation the clear width of the supply and exhaust openings in opposite exterior walls must be extremely large and should be at least 0.1 to 0.2 m² per m² floor area. Depending on the room height this amounts to between 40 and 80 per cent of the total wall surface area of the space. The buildings should therefore be designed in a way that is very open to the wind and the movement of air. In traditional buildings the exterior walls were often made of simple woven bamboo that provided a visual screen, as the examples in this book show. Today, for reasons of noise insulation alone, solutions of this kind have a limited applicability. Where possible, the depth of the space should not exceed five times its height (bottom right). Partition walls at right angles to the flow of air should be avoided, as these increase the flow resistance and hinder the passage of air. Given the frequency of severe storms it must be possible to regulate the supply and exhaust flow in an adequate way, that is to say, exhaust and supply openings must be closable, in particular in areas prone to typhoons.

Intensive ventilation is also necessary to maintain and protect buildings in the warm and humid climatic zone from deterioration by water from perspiration. The constant high relative air humidity means that, in contrast to the warm and dry climatic zone, the dew-point temperature is generally very close to the air temperature. Even slight differences in temperature between air and surface temperature of the building's structure, or of the fittings, can lead to the temperature falling below dew point, causing condensation on the surfaces as well as attack by algae and the growth of mould. Therefore the of all building elements, as well as the fittings, must be constantly well aired. Above all, cavities or voids should not be created unless they can be adequately ventilated.

For this reason – unlike the situation obtaining in the warm and dry climate – the building elements must be as light as possible and should store no or only very little heat, as the storage of heat dampens the course of the surface temperatures and shifts

its peak temporally compared with air temperature, thereby increasing the danger of condensation. Thus, for the warm and humid climatic zone the most suitable mode of construction is lightweight construction, which, in general, is the most unsuitable for other climatic zones (at least from the viewpoint of building climatology). However, particular attention must be paid to providing sufficient thermal insulation, especially in those parts of the building that are exposed to direct sunshine. Where possible, these building parts should be constructed of two separate, well-ventilated layers, as already described in the case of the warm and dry climatic zone.

If a mechanical climate control is envisaged from the start – for instance, because optimal interior climatic conditions must be ensured in a housing block for reasons of comfort, or because the technology used in a production building sets very stringent limits on the interior climate that are impossible to meet by natural means of climate control – then the design

Open, cross-ventilated urban concept of a coastal town in Togo

naturally ventilated buildings	criteria	air-conditioned buildings
scattered	urban pattern	dense
open coverage type	building design & construction	closed coverage type
> max.!	ventilation rate	> min.!
> 0!	thermal capacity	> 0!
irrelevant (if shaded)	thermal insulation	necessary
as large as possible	openings	as small as possible
whole building envelope (esp. roof)	shading	whole building envelope (esp. roof)
rain (esp. driving rain) and rising moisture	moisture protection	rain (esp. driving rain) rising moisture and water vapour diffusion

Table 1: Comparison of main design principles for naturally-ventilated buildings and air-conditioned buildings under warm and humid climate conditions

of the building must follow quite different design criteria. To reduce the expense of air-conditioning as far as possible, an air-conditioned building should always (and in every climatic zone) be almost completely sealed off from the exterior climate. For the warm and humid climatic zone this means that, in addition to the necessary sun protection, the shell of the building must not only be completely thermally insulated but also windproof and airtight. The problem of diffusion of water vapour must also be dealt with, as, in contrast to a climate controlled by natural means, in a building with air-conditioning the water vapour pressure of the inside air can lie considerably below that of the outside air, thus causing water vapour to flow from outside to inside. In such a case the external construction must be extremely carefully planned and built and, under certain circumstances, should incorporate an external vapour barrier.

Table 1, which compiles and contrasts these fundamental design principles, clearly shows that in the warm and humid climatic zone in particular it is impossible to 'repair' a building that has been poorly or inadequately planned (as regards the principles of natural climate control) simply by installing an air-conditioning system – without significant curtailments in the area of energy efficiency and, therefore, economy.

Therefore, the parameters of the indoor climate to be observed must be clearly determined at the very beginning of the planning process. At the same time it must be decided whether these are to be met by the use of natural climate control or with mechanical air-conditioning. Only then, as has been shown above, can a basic building model emerge that can serve as a basis for urban and architectural planning.

Main principles of climatically appropriate building in the warm and humid tropics

Settlement and urban structure

These include a spacious urban concept that are open to wind and air movement as much as possible. Preference should be given to sites on hilltops, slopes, coastlines or the edge of larger lakes. Streets should be even and comparatively wide, oriented to the prevailing wind direction and planted with tall trees for shading purposes. Lower bushes and shrubs close to houses should be avoided as they obstruct efficient ventilation.

A development of tall, approximately point-shaped buildings arranged in a chequerboard urban pattern is preferable to a development of elongated, closed rows of buildings.

Building typology

This includes a preference for lightweight (frame) constructions. Houses should be set on pillars and raised above ground. External walls should be designed as open as possible to let the wind in and to allow as much movement of air and ventilation within the houses as possible. The building should be shaded by trees, wind-open mats, screens or blinds (*brise-soleils*).

The main façade should preferably be placed across the prevailing wind direction and, if possible, orientated from south-south-east to south-south-west (in the northern hemisphere) or from north-north-east to north-north-west (in the southern hemisphere).

Building design and construction

Rooms, preferably arranged side-by-side to allow cross-ventilation, are best accessed from an external passageway. The open sequence of rooms must not have internal corridors or partitions which would form a barrier, and stairs should be placed externally at gable ends. This allows for cross-ventilation of the connected spaces, which, as a result of the cooling effect of transpiration evaporating from the body,

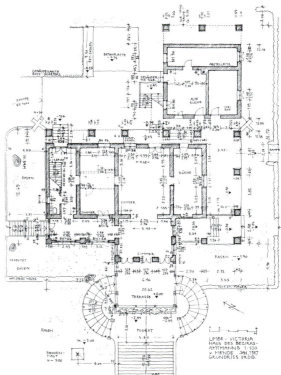

A German colonial building in Limbe, Cameroon, with a seperate
kitchen at the lee side of the building away from the sea breezes
to avoid cooking fumes from entering the house.

A climatically appropriate living area in a bungalow hotel in
Cameroon with a deep projecting eaves and shady veranda
(opposite page)

108

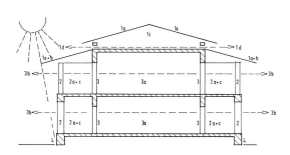

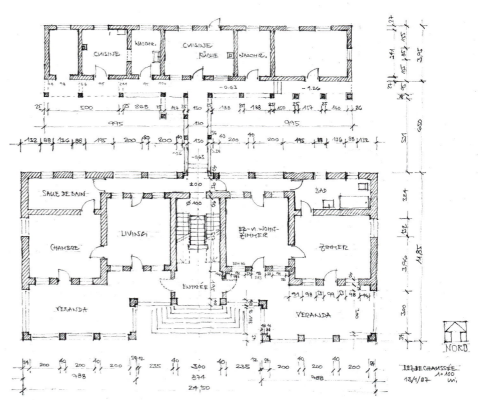

The urban planning of Rio de Janeiro (top) was devised in such a way that cooling sea breezes provided natural ventilation of the city.

The principal of natural cross-ventilation was utilized by German colonial architects in the coastal city of Douala, Cameroon (see pages 6–7).

110

A new administrative building (1987) in Cameroon: the building lacks all concept of natural climate control and its façades are mistakenly oriented in an east-west direction.

Open, cross-ventilated living space in the humid coastal region of western Cameron

allows for tolerable climatic conditions in the rooms. The movement of air can be supported by a fan. The shaded and well-ventilated access passageways can also be used as loggias or verandas, which further enhance the quality of life in the dwelling. No differentiation should be made between windows and wall-openings; openings should be designed as large as possible, be well shaded and protected against rainwater. Roofs should be steep with projecting ends to protect the outer walls from both sun and rain.

A preference should be given to well-ventilated, double-layer roofconstructions. External surfaces should be in light pastel colours in order to reflect solar radiation and minimise the absorption of heat.

1   K. Ferstl, *Zur Stellung bauklimatischer Faktoren im Gesamt- system architektonischen Gestaltens – Die Herausbildung einer energetisch motivierten Architekturkonzeption*, Dresden, 1992.
2   *Annual Energy Review 2002*, Energy Information Administra- tion, Washington, D.C., October 2003.
3   *International Energy Annual 2001*, Energy Information Ad- ministration, Washington, D.C.
4   K. Petzold, 'Klima', in: Lutz, Jenisch, Klopfer, et al., *Lehrbuch der Bauphysik*, Stuttgart, 1997.
5   H. Rietsche, W. Raiß, *Lehrbuch der Heizungs- und Lüftungs- technik*, Berlin, 1968.
6   M. Rubner, *Zur Bilanz unserer Wärmeökonomie*, 1896, p. 69.
7   P.O. Fanger, *Thermal comfort – Analysis and Applications in Environmental Engineering*, Copenhagen, 1970.
8   J. Dreyfuß, *Le comfort dans l'habitation en pays tropical*, Paris, 1960.
9   W. Böer, *Technische Meteorologie*, Leipzig 1964.
10 K. Petzold, *Bauen in warmen Klimaten – bauklimatische Grund- lagen*, Leipzig, 1986.
11 K. Petzold, R. Hoinka, *Einfache Verfahren zur Bemessung des Wärmeschutzes von Wohnbauten in warmen Klimaten*, Weimar, 1987, pp. 153 ff.
12 K. Ferstl, *Zu einigen Grundprinzipien des Bauens in außer- europäischen Klimazonen*, Dresden, n.d., pp. 39 ff.
13 Koenigsberger, et al., *Manuel of Tropical Housing and Building*, London 1973.

Building materials in the Tropics
Wolfgang Lauber

Building in the Tropics means for both the builder and designer a constructive confrontation with extreme climatic conditions.

- ► In the hot and humid zones, high humidity levels in conjunction with the constant heat represent a major problem for materials and construction. In

  the case of organic materials these conditions lead to swelling, and in the case of metals, to increased corrosion that can take the form of rust or oxidation.

- ► In coastal regions the salty air of the coastal winds intensifies these processes. Even metals with protected surfaces, such as galvanised iron, anodised aluminium, stainless steel, coated metal sections, as well as concrete surfaces, are subject to extreme attack. The high humidity level also creates problems for wood and other organic building materials, for example, fungus, microbes and insects, termites, and other pests.

  Strong gusts of wind during typhoons and storms in the rainy season impose considerable tension and compression forces on structures, while erosion caused by heavy rainfall is another major problem.

  The use of friction-type joints and junctions in construction and detailing is therefore of particular importance.

- ► In the hot and dry zone the most significant problems are those caused by solar radiation and UV rays etc. These can destroy surface finishes, above all coated surfaces of metal sections, metal sheeting, plastic panels and wood surfaces. The great temperature differences, with daytime temperatures of 45 °C in the summer and cold winter nights with temperatures below freezing point,

impose considerable strain on construction and materials in the form of swelling and contraction. Sand-bearing winds can have a damaging effect on surface finishes, such as sandblasted surfaces. Particularly susceptible are glass surfaces, galvanised and anodised metals, coatings and plastics and also hard building materials, such as fair-faced concrete, cement-bound sandstone, clay bricks and external render.

- ► Biological pests

  In the Tropics, biological pests represent a dangerous plague that is often extremely difficult to combat. These include insects such as termites, midges and flies, as well as rats, mice and fungi. Termites represent the greatest danger for all organic building materials. Of the roughly 1,800 known kinds of termite, around 100 are regarded as a threat to buildings. Earth termites can climb through cracks and joints to reach the timber elements in a building. Flying termites nest in wood and destroy it by building channels and cavities. Organic building materials, such as thermal insulation materials, textiles, leather, rubber and foam materials, are all susceptible to attack. All hard building materials, such as concrete, masonry, stone, mortar and metals, cannot be attacked, but they can be soiled by the pap the termites leave when hollowing out their channels.

  Buildings can be protected by the proper choice of materials, such as termite-resistant woods containing high amounts of tannin, resins or essential oils, plywood panels bound with synthetic resin or by chemical protection. Before they are used in a building, wooden parts can be sprayed or immersed in solutions of metallic salts (copper sulphates, zinc oxides, borate salt or creosote), which should be applied, above all, to any cracks, joints and freshly cut areas. Constructional measures, such as projecting termite flashings on load-bearing columns, are, generally speaking, ineffectual.

- Protection against mosquitoes and flies
  The only way to combat the problem of insects and reduce the danger of infections, such as malaria, carried by the anopheles fly, is to seal windows and door openings with mesh screens made of stainless steel or plastic and positioned in front of the frames.
- The most effective protection against fungus resulting primarily from high humidity is provided by damp-proofing and proper ventilation of the building

Traditional and modern building materials

The choice of building materials is essentially determined by their local availability, their economy, durability and suitability for the particular climate. The means of transporting materials from a distant place of production must be taken into consideration. In addition, for many people, above all in the tropical megacity regions, the acceptance of a material is related to its status. The hut made of clay, wood or bamboo is rejected by most of the new, poor, city dwellers as they long to build with the materials of the rich: concrete, brick and natural stone, steel, glass and shiny metal.

The extent to which they can be worked by hand by local craftsmen and unskilled workers is a further influential factor in the choice of building materials.

Construction timber

Suitable building timber is available in almost all tropical climatic regions, nowadays also in the form of prefabricated plywood.

The construction methods used can include skeletal frame, platform frame or prefabricated systems with panels.

The use of hardwoods guarantees resistance to the problems provided by the climate. Care must be taken to protect timber properly by keeping timber building elements dry, protecting them against ground damp by means of plinths or by raising the building and protecting façade elements through the use of projecting roofs.

In the hot and humid Tropics, and above all in the salty air of the coastal areas, only rustproof V4A stainless-steel connections, cast-steel elements or traditional timber joints should be used. To combat fungus attack, metal salt solutions can be used, while construction methods that keep the structure dry are also useful in combatting this problem. Timber that contains tannin and resin – such as the ronier palm (Borassus athiopia) in West and North Africa, all hard redwoods, such as kaicedra, different kinds of mahogany, macaranduba, afzelia, the various acacias, tamarisk and teak – are all resistant to termites (information supplied by the Institute for Building Materials Research in the University in Kumasi, Ghana).

Building with bamboo

Bamboo buildings are widely found in traditional architecture wherever the bamboo grass flourishes in regions of Africa, South America and, above all, South-East Asia. This widespread, fast-growing building material is extremely economical, comes in long lengths and offers a multitude of economic advantages. It has a low self-weight, is highly resistant to tension and compression forces and bending moments and is easy to work without the need for specialist skills, which makes it particularly suitable for buildings that the poor construct themselves. Bamboo tends to rot relatively quickly but this process can be prevented or at least reduced by conservation methods such as watering regularly, smoking, or treating with mineral salts. Protecting buildings against the weather by means of deep roof

The transportation of wood in Africa (above left); a modern
timber-frame construction using V2A bolts (above right);
students making traditional tenon timber joints (bottom left),
using resources from the tropical rainforest (bottom right)

projections, keeping the plinth area dry by elevating the building, or constructing a solid stone plinth all represent important contributions to extending the lifespan of bamboo architecture.

The relatively low status of bamboo buildings, which are generally viewed as the architecture of the poor, can be raised by formal improvements in terms of architectural design. This is shown in a highly impressive manner by the buildings of the Colombian architect Simon Vélez, who designed a spectacular building, the Ceri Pavilion, to represent his native country at the Hanover World Fair in 2000.

Bamboo is one of the most widely used plants in the world; around 1,500 different kinds in 75 different species cover about 25 million hectares in tropical and subtropical zones around the world, while about 10 per cent of the plants grow in temperate zones. Bamboo is also one of the world's fastest growing plants, with many kinds growing by as much as one metre in a day. Each kind of bamboo reaches its maximum cane length in between two to three months. In a moderate climate this length is around two to five metres; in the case of tropical bamboos it ranges between 20 and 30 metres. After a growing period of four to five years bamboo is mature enough to be used for building purposes.

China is the world's leading producer of bamboo. The advantage of bamboo is that it it spreads through its root system, which means that the plant begins to grow again immediately after harvesting. By contrast, it requires considerable effort and expense to build up a normal wood again after all the trees have been felled.

Bamboo can be used and processed at every phase of its growth cycle. First of all, as bamboo shoots (30 days), then for baskets and woven goods (six months to one year), while two-year-old bamboo canes can be split and woven together in strips. Once the bamboo is three years old it can be used for construction purposes, but the optimum age is around five years. Bamboo should not, however, be older than six years as its rigidity begins to decrease from this age onwards. Generally, bamboo is cut in the early morning when the moon is in its last quarter as this is the time when its moisture content is at a minimum. Nevertheless, after the harvest and quality control, bamboo must be stored for two to three months until it has lost about 90 per cent of its moisture content.

The major disadvantage of bamboo is its vulnerability to attack by insects, fungus and fire. Methods of treating bamboo to deal with these problems include, for example, watering it, lime-washing, removal of moisture by smoking, and heating, whereby the bamboo releases its pyrolytic acids when warmed gently. This process makes the surface smoother and more resistant to fire.

Not only the bamboo canes are used. The stalks, for example, can be split into bamboo lathes – the most common form in which bamboo is used – and bamboo beading can be used to make mats, baskets, furniture or semi-finished industrial products. Other products include pressboard made of compressed bamboo sawdust, laminates made of bamboo or that have similar properties to that of normal wood (chipboard) but are considerably more elastic.

Lightweight protection from the sun: cut from bamboo and used by a Fulbe nomad woman on a dromedary (top left). Other examples of how bamboo can be used for construction and furniture (centre), as well as for traditional and modern jointing methods (bottom)

Opposite page: modern bamboo buildings by Colombian architect Simon Vélez (top left) and one of hundreds of bamboo types (top right) commonly used in building (bottom).

Construction

Bamboo is frequently used in South-East Asia for the construction of bridges, houses and also as scaffolding in the construction industry.

Simple junctions can be made using bamboo fibres up to a metre long that are tied together; more complex junctions involve using screws, whereby the bamboo must be partly filled with concrete to prevent it from ripping.

As bamboo wood tends to shrink, the junctions used in bamboo buildings must be elastic, which involves using hardwood bolts and diagonal connections, elastic fibres made of bamboo or plastic thread that is resistant to ageing. Rigid connections using screws or iron wire are generally unsuitable.

Steel, cast iron, aluminium and copper

Steel
These materials, which are generally imported, are used in the form of reinforcement steel, construction steel sections, cast-steel parts and metal sheeting, often as galvanised corrugated iron. Corrosion of untreated steel and iron is a major problem, particularly in the hot and humid zones. The high salt content of the air in coastal regions (where most of the construction in the megacities takes place nowadays) is an important additional factor. Protective measures include painting, heat-dried coating, dipping or hot galvanising.

In the case of stainless steel, V4A quality (molybdenum alloy) should be used in coastal regions or V3a chrome-nickel steel.

Aluminium
Although this raw material is found the Tropics, aluminium products are generally manufactured in industrialised countries on account of the considerable amount of energy used in the electrolysing process. Aluminium sheeting has a reflective quality that can lead to unpleasant and annoying reflections, above all in rural settlement areas, where it is used on pitched roofs.

The use of steel, cast iron, aluminium and copper in the Tropics: an old steel bridge (top left) built in Cameroon during the colonial era (1908); a jetty in Lomé (bottom right) corroded by seawater (1912); corrugated aluminium roofing on small bamboo houses (top right); steel is used to build a modern-day factory (centre right). The hotel (bottom left) on the coast of Togo has an aluminium curtain-wall façade that is resistant to sea water.

Protection against corrosion is provided by the natural oxidation of the surface. This can be improved by the use of alloy additives (magnesium). This treatment is especially recommended for the aluminium sections used in window frames and in façade construction in coastal areas, where the air has a high salt content.

Additional surface protection can be provided by powder coatings and anodising.

Copper
This raw material is also found in the Tropics. It is produced above all in rolled bands for use as a corrosion-resistant sheeting. The protective layer of patina that results from oxidation occurs sooner in the hot and humid zones of the Tropics. Reference should be made here to the bactericidal properties of copper. In the chemical methods of protecting timber, a saline copper solution is used to combat fungus, bacteria and termites.

Glass
In the Tropics, glass is generally an expensive imported material. Glazing façade openings makes sense only when rooms must be protected against dust (museums, health care facilities) or if they are completely air-conditioned.

In hot and dry zones, the use of solar-protection glass can make sense, above all for high-level glazing and roof lights to reduce the build-up of radiant heat.

In regions with dust-bearing winds or heavy rainfall, reflective sun protective films are unsuitable as they tend to weather badly.

The variation represented by the horizontally adjustable glass louvre window, the so-called fenêtre persienne, offers the advantage that it allows rooms to be completely ventilated while protecting them against such problems as dust-bearing winds or squalls of rain.

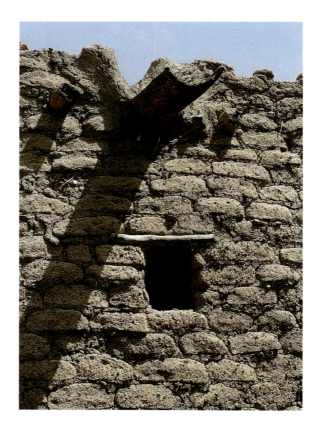

Clay and fired brick

The building material clay is available in sufficient amounts and in good quality across wide areas of the Tropics. In Africa and Latin America in particular, the mix of weathered geological granite base rock with the sand that gets blown in produces a very stable clay that has been used for ceramic products and, above all, for bricks or roof tiles for thousands of years.

In the hot and dry zones, unfired clay structures are made 'in Banco' (torus technique) with air-dried clay bricks or rammed clay construction.

The danger of weathering during the rainy season means that the external skin should be protected by rendering. Resistance to weathering can be greatly improved by the use of organic additives or cement. Nevertheless, traditional clay architecture remains 'an architecture of transience' that requires regular maintenance after one to three rainy seasons.

Its susceptibility to mechanical damage when wet requires a hard protective base or plinth made of stonework.

Clay structures offer good thermal insulation, which makes them particularly suitable for building in the hot and dry climatic zone. Clay buildings are, by and large, resistant to attack by microbes and parasites, as the extremely dry clay base does not offer any dampness, which such parasites require. Adding cement to the clay bricks or to the internal plastering can reduce the likelihood of termite attacks.

The advantageous climatic behaviour of clay architecture as produced by traditional, labour-intensive handmade methods can no longer be used to meet the demand for dwellings in the megacities in the Tropics. This construction method remains widespread only in rural areas.

An example of a building with rammed-clay walls.

Opposite page: traditional rendered-clay walls built using the Banco technique on a plinth of natural stone (top left), which protects against erosion; the production of air-dried clay bricks (top right) to the widely-used dimensions of 40 x 20 x 10 cm; a wall being built using the cob technique (bottom left). A traditional clay-built mosque (bottom right) in Mali dating from the 12th century

124

The industrial production of sand-cement blocks for walls and hollow-element floor slabs (above left) is very widespread in tropical countries. Solid sand-cement blocks without any insulating cavities are unsuitable as they offer insufficient thermal insulation. A typical frame structure with concrete corner columns and infill walls built of sand-cement blocks (bottom) without insulation against heating by the sun. A small museum and cultural centre (top right) in Dogon country, Mali, built with natural stone; clay bricks are used for interior insulation (see page 157).

Natural stone

In the hot and dry zones, natural stone is a suitable material for constructing plinths for clay buildings to resist erosion or for external walls requiring little maintenance. Its use is advantageous only in regions where it is found locally, as the transport of this heavy material is expensive and working it is also costly. Stone offers little thermal insulation but when combined with insulating or fired hollow or clay bricks in the form of a double-shell structure it can provide a highly suitable and functional concept.

Sand-cement blocks

The use of sand-cement blocks for walls and ceiling slabs is very widespread in tropical countries. In their production simple forms are often used in an amateur self-build process. This method of production is hardly suitable, however, for walls that must carry heavier loads for, in contrast to industrial production methods, the blocks are not pressed in the moulds. Furthermore, mixes low in cement (< 1:4) and sand with a high salt content are frequently used, which has resulted, above all in coastal regions, in premature decay (disintegration) of the blocks. On account of this, these blocks are frequently used only as infill material in concrete frame buildings. If they are not used in the form of cavity blocks, which offer better thermal insulation, but merely as solid blocks with a minimal thickness of 10 cm, then the interiors heat up excessively because the solid blocks radiate the energy they have stored during the day until late in the evening. Economic hollow-element systems for building floor slabs are available in many tropical countries. Cement-bound hollow blocks or bricks are laid between prefabricated concrete T-beams and then covered with a 6- to 8-cm screed reinforced with steel reinforcement mats. This produces stable, quickly erected floor slabs with spans of up to around 5 metres at a low cost.

Concrete and reinforced concrete

The production of reinforced concrete is by now widespread in most tropical countries, even in remote regions. However, even a minimum standard is often not achieved because of efforts to economise by using sand-cement mixes of less than 1 to 5 and the frequent use of dirty additives for water and sand (humus, coastal sand), or because the formwork is removed prematurely in the hot and humid climatic regions during high daytime temperatures. In areas with little timber, concrete columns are inserted between the previously erected blockwork walls, with a thickness of 10 to 15 cm, using flat board shuttering.

The reinforcement is often insufficient and the columns too slender, which leads to the collapse of buildings several storeys high, above all in those cases where the concrete work is not carried out by skilled workers.

The corrosion of the reinforcement steel where the concrete cover is less than 3 cm is also a particular danger.

Concrete has high thermal storage properties and low thermal insulation and should therefore be carefully protected against heating when it comes to incorporating design elements that shade it from the sun.

Plastics and films

Plastics have established themselves in the Tropics, too, generally in the form of imported industrial products. However, where it is planned to use them in façades and roofs, their resistance to weathering and to UV light should be examined. Frequently, plastic surfaces become dry and brittle as a result of strong solar radiation.

Insulating foils and films should have a reinforcing mesh and, above all in flat roofs, they should be protected by screeds, a layer of gravel, or ceramic slabs that can be walked across.

Lightweight construction panels and woven mats

In tropical countries, pressed panels bound with cement or synthetic resin and made of organic raw materials, such as wood fibre, or of agricultural waste products, such as rice husks, coconut shells, etc., are available for the fitting out and completion of interiors. Traditionally woven mats made of bamboo, palm leaves, palm panicles, grass and similar plant materials are also used in new buildings to erect light canopy roofs that offer shade against the sun or as transparent lightweight partition walls, especially in hot and humid climates.

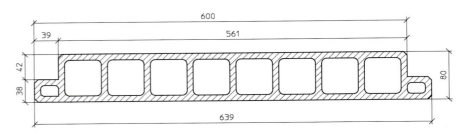

Clay building panels, 3E panel system

A new development in the area of construction is the industrially produced panel building system from the German company Händle GmbH in Mühlacker, near Stuttgart. Here, the raw material clay is mixed with recycled waste products, such as straw, wood fibre, etc., as well as with a small amount of cement and additives. Using extrusion technology, this mix is pressed to form large, lightweight panels with a width of 60 cm and lengths up to a full storey which are then dried without the use of energy. In this process, far less primary energy is used than in firing bricks or making cement for the production of concrete and yet, thanks to the density of the panel material, it is stable, fire-resistant, waterproof and can be easily fixed by screwing. In addition, the panels can be produced in different thicknesses and with insulating cavities, according to the particular mouthpiece used in the extrusion process.

In the Tropics, fired bricks are generally only lightly fired (below 700 °C), are only 10 cm thick and are therefore generally suitable only as infill in skeletal frame buildings, where they are plastered over. This construction method is today widespread in the Tropics. However, it does have serious disadvantages as regards thermal insulation and thermal storage, particularly in the hot and dry climatic zone, and is more suitable as a lightweight system in hot and humid climatic regions. The high constructive expenditure is due to the use of energy for cement, building steel and bricks, which makes such buildings expensive. The advantage of this simple construction system lies in the fact that it can be erected using unskilled workers.

Use of the Händle clay building panels on different building sites in Thailand and Australia

Environmental Protection through insulation systems in the Tropics

In tropical climate zones, protecting the outer walls of a building from the sun's heat is an important constructive method to ensure a comfortable interior climate and good ventilation, as well as to reduce the energy usage in airconditioned structures.

In the future, the price of energy around the world will rise dramatically, to a large extent because of a predicted 60 per cent rise in the demand for energy in the developing countries of the Tropics during the next 20 years. In addition, increased demands for environmental protection and quality in the design of building interiors will lead to increased interest in energy saving insulation techniques.

Insulation systems have been widely used in building in the US and in Europe, and are distributed worldwide by the company Sto AG based in Stuehlingen, Germany. This system is an economically efficient method for heat containment with only a marginal loss ratio.

Single-layered construction in tropical regions is also a traditional building method in which both the load-carrying and heat-containment capacities of the walls are combined.

This construction method has in recent decades continued to develop throughout the world into the single-frame construction method. It is especially prevalent in the anonymous building structures in the emerging world, which usually consist of concrete supports between which walls with insufficient strength or heat containment capacity are placed. This reliable insulation method is well suited to improve the heat containment capacities of single-frame structures in the Tropics, however, the high humidity in these regions must be taken into account. Extensive hydrothermal examinations should be undertaken before the use of the system in order to adapt the construction method or building materials (such as vapour-tight plaster and insulating materials).

The advantages of this construction method include effective protection from precipitation, the greater storage capacity of large building elements and their crack-free surfaces through the mechanical separation of the building elements.

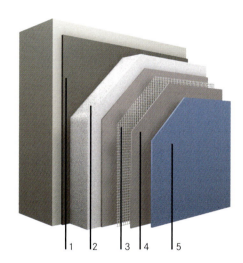

1   Adhesive
2   Insulation board
3   Reinforcing coat
4   Glassfibre mesh
5   Finish coat

Façade insulation system
by the company Sto AG

New Approaches to a Climatically Appropriate and Humane Architecture in the Tropics

The Museum of Contemporary Art, Niterói, near Rio de Janeiro, by Oscar Niemeyer

The former Governor's Palace (top) in Lomé, Togo, completed in 1905: a functional design with restrained decoration. An elevated German house (centre) in the coastal region of Cameroon. Climatic protection of the façade is provided by the wide projections of the roof (centre and bottom).

Colonial architecture: a first step towards a new architecture for new functions

In the 19th century, international economic liberalism encouraged the development of an export industry that required considerable amounts of raw materials that had to be found more easily and cheaply than on the world market.

In addition, new outlet markets and new lands that could absorb emigration were sought in response to concerns about the overpopulation of Europe.

An important factor may also have been the fascination that the 'exotic' quality of distant tropical lands exerted upon bourgeois society.

These developments were recognised by the leading trading companies at the beginning of the 19th century. They founded trading posts on the coasts of Africa and Asia through which a busy trade in both raw materials and finished products was conducted. The competition among the Europeans who traded along the coasts was so intense that by the mid-century the various national governments had begun to stake their interests in colonies of their own, a process that was finally regulated by the Berlin Conference of 1884.

The engineers built roads, bridges, railways, drainage systems and harbours that are still in existence today.

The architects built schools, hospitals, administrative buildings and dwelling houses that have been well preserved and many of which are still used. European scientists conducted research into the fauna and flora, geology and geography of the tropical countries. Planters laid out plantations that today still produce crops and, with the help of botanists, introduced new kinds of plants and crops to produce coffee, tea, oil (from palm trees), bananas and spices.

Postal and telegraph systems, railways and shipping all functioned trouble-free.

This school in Togo (1912) includes a teacher's apartment. Originally the building was an example of consistent, climatically appropriate design. Today, unfortunately, the former veranda has been enclosed.

► The long axis of the building runs east-west
► The internal 'core' spaces with their solid walls are reached from a continuous veranda running outside them, thus allowing north-south cross-ventilation of the living spaces
► Ventilation of the roof as a buffer space
► The light colour of the exterior increases the degree of reflection

After 1900, architecture had to confront new kinds of building tasks that resulted from the colonists' importation of European lifestyles. Administrative buildings, schools, hospitals, sport and leisure facilities, libraries and museums, transport facilities such as railway stations, airfields and seaports, factories and new kinds of housing were all required.

A first start was made by the colonial buildings erected by the European powers, which offer many appropriately designed examples but are sometimes burdened with the typical eclectic decoration of the late 19th and early 20th centuries.

However, a shortage of materials and lack of skilled building workers often led to astonishingly modern buildings without the heavy ornate decoration of European architecture of the time.

A particularly remarkable feature is the global 'internationalism' of colonial buildings in all tropical regions, from South America to Africa to South-East Asia because, after the Berlin Conference, the European colonial powers agreed to divide up the Tropics among themselves and in many fields, including building construction and design, they worked together and exchanged the benefits of their experience.

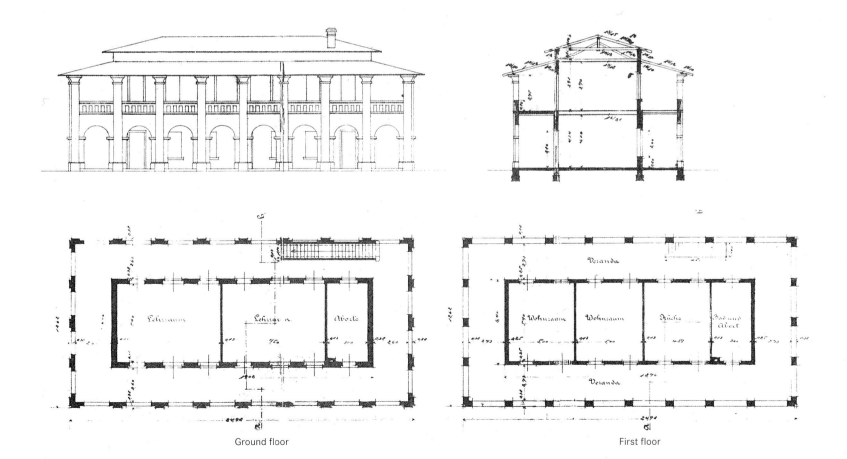

Ground floor   First floor

**German colonial architecture in Cameroon,
West Africa**

Palace of King Manga Bell, in Douala, built in 1912
in 'pagoda style' with lightweight loggias in front and
the roof as an open protective covering (right);
Divisional office in Limbe, Cameroon: the former
'district office' and the 'Palaver Building' (top), built
by the Germans after 1890. An interesting 'house-in-
house' construction. A lightweight steel-frame roof
tops a stone building with emphasised corners.
Open loggias and a staircase placed at the gable end
provide access to the 'inner' house. Cross-ventilation and loggias protect the core of the building from
the worst of the heat.

**English colonial architecture in the coastal region
of Accra, Ghana**

Hospital with open ground floor: the sick station
on the upper floor is well ventilated by winds from
the sea and has a veranda in front to provide shade
(centre). Ventilated roof space, light, reflective
colours used externally.

Colonial architecture in Brazil
This bank building (left) in Rio de Janeiro displays climatically responsive input in the form of projecting, shady loggias and roofed-over, open alcoves. The photograph below shows a typical example of hacienda-style architecture in Brazil in 1926.

134

German colonial architecture in China

A longing for the distant native country led to the use of the representational 'Kaiser Wilhelm style' of the late 19th and early 20th centuries.

The richly decorated buildings are evidence of the prosperity of the people who built them and, in contrast to the situation in Africa, they also indicate the existence of skilled Chinese building workers who were able to reproduce in far-off China the 'granite-loving' architecture of the era of Kaiser Wilhelm II. However, these buildings rarely show indications of climatically appropriate construction.

The former Governor's Palace in Tsingtau (centre), with striking granite façade elements (top); it was completed in 1907.

The former ambassador's summer residence (bottom), 1908. The formal design of this house is comparable to the German colonial house in southern Cameroon (see. p. 107). The functionally correct use of verandas in front of the main spaces provide shade.

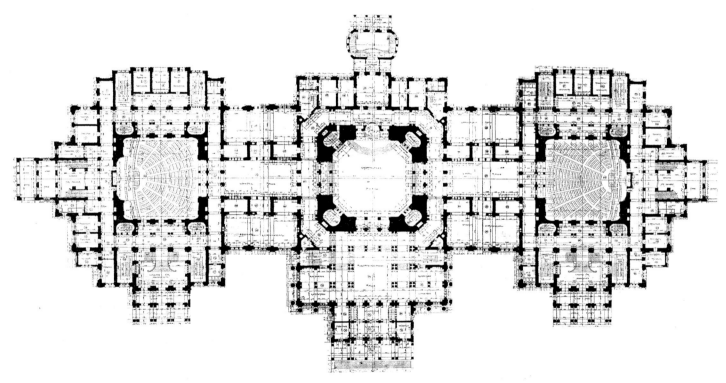

Chinese Parliament Building, Beijing, by the German architect Curt Rothkegel, who described the structure as 'a building approximately twice the size of the Reichstag in Berlin', that had been completed in 1894. Rothkegel's design for Beijing is far broader and, in response to the planned constitution of the government, has three domes: Emperor – Lower House – Upper House. Construction was stopped in 1914.

French colonial architecture in Phnom-Penh, Cambodia
The above example of a global architecture at the turn of the previous century shows sensible signs of a climatically appropriate concept: roofed loggias, the correct east-west orientation of the building and cross-ventilation of the shaded core walls by means of external circulation routes.

Colonial architecture in South-East Asia and Oceania
Elevating the ground floor on a plinth or on piers, as illustrated in the photographs on the opposite page, improves the ventilation of the living rooms on the upper floor and ensures that the spaces on the ground are kept dry.

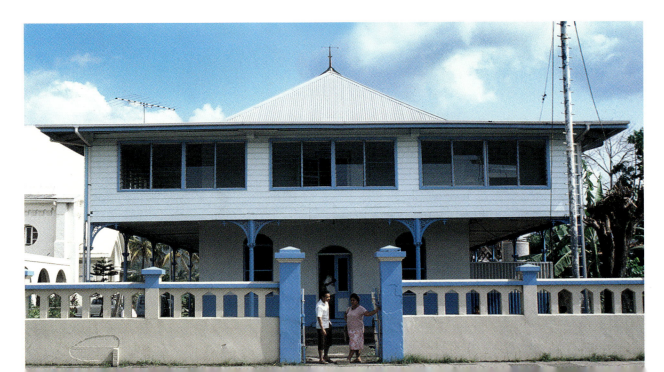

138 The contribution of modern architecture and its encounter with traditional and vernacular architecture

The first forward-pointing contributions to climatically appropriate building in the Tropics were made by leading architects of Modernism, although many of their efforts were marred by serious defects. Above all, Le Corbusier and his Brazilian partners and colleagues Lucio Costa, Oscar Niemeyer and Affonso Eduardo Reidy, as well as the American architect Louis Kahn, demonstrated with their buildings in Brazil and India how a modern architecture that is based on an ecological concept of providing protection from the climate can be achieved.

Modernist architects recognised the lessons that could be learned from traditional architecture in the tropical regions. The further study of the forms of colonial architecture in Latin America, Asia and Africa helped them to understand the climatically-influenced principles employed there and to use them in the creation of a new Modernism suited to the Tropics.

Above all in early 20th-century Brazil, which was still a young country at the time, a fruitful dialogue conducted with the leading European Bauhaus architects and their 'brothers in faith', such as Le Corbusier, led to the creation of a regional architecture that remains most impressive today. The leading personalities, such as Niemeyer, Reidy and Costa, established a new Brazilian architecture movement. From the wealth of remarkable buildings they created a number are mentioned below *pars pro toto*.

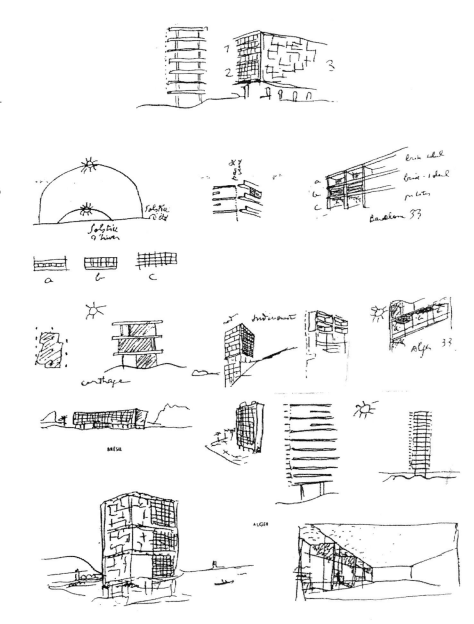

Ideas sketched by Le Corbusier on how to build in the hot climatic zone of the Tropics

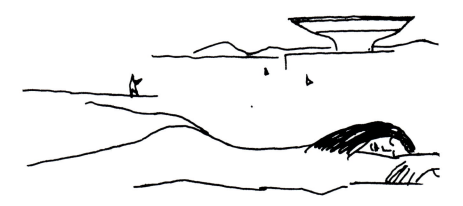

"I am not attracted to straight angles or to the straight lines, hard and inflexible, created by man.
I am attracted to free-flowing sensual curves. The curves that I find in the mountains of my country, in the sinuousness of its rivers, in the waves of the ocean, and on the body of the beloved woman. Curves make up the entire Universe, the curved Universe of Einstein."
(*The Poet of the Line*, Oscar Niemeyer)

Museum of Contemporary Art in Rio de Janeiro, 1999

Architect: Oscar Niemeyer
This central plan building is strikingly positioned on a rocky promontory above the beach of Niteró. The view of the bay of Rio from the external circulation ramp is most impressive. The outward sloping façade of the circular building is turned away from the sun and towards the view. This reduces the heating up of the air-conditioned museum space and consequently also cuts running costs. The air-conditioning plant is housed in the buffered, two-layer roof space and must cope with Rio's hot and humid climate and maintain constant temperatures and humidity levels in the interior. The white colour used externally reflects solar radiation.

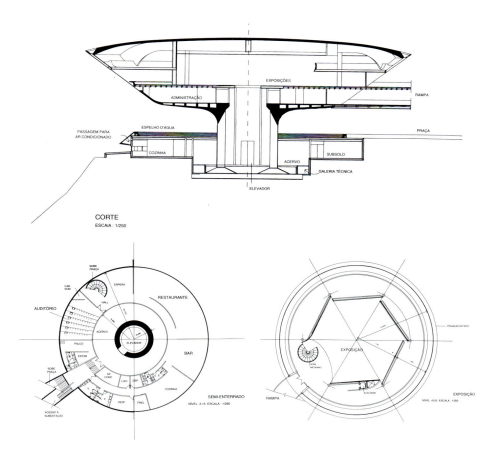

The Museum of Modern Art, Rio de Janeiro, Brazil, 1958
Architect: Affonso Eduardo Reidy
Adapted to the local climate, this building is cooled through its plinth structure from below and the wide projecting roof that provides shade from the high southern sun.

Buildings for Brasilia, Brazil, 1956
Architekt: Oscar Niemeyer
New Government Building (above)
National Congress (below)
Closed forms are used for the large central spaces
and there is an optimal east-west orientation of the
twin office blocks (below).

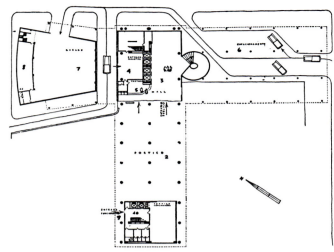

142 **Ministry of Education and Health, Rio de Janeiro,
1936–37**

Architects: Lucio Costa, Le Corbusier and Oscar
Niemeyer

The urban placing of the building with its long axis
running east-west is climatically correct. The cross-
ventilation made possible by the two-storey eleva-
tion is climatically correct too, but the organisation
of the office spaces along a central corridor (see
plans right) prevents the essential cross-ventilation
of the workspaces, something that Le Corbusier had
proposed for an administration building in Algiers
(below).

Ground floor:
2 Portico
3 Public hall
4 Minister's entrance
5 Information desk
6 Parking
7 Garage
8 Machinery
9, 10 Employees' entrance

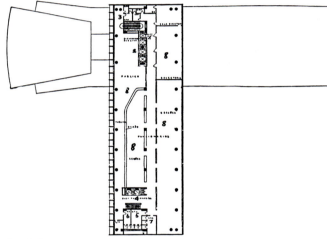

Fourth floor:
1 Minister's lift
2 Public elevator
3 Toilet
4 Employees' lift
5, 7 Toilets
8 Office space

House of Agriculture in São Paulo, 1955   143
Architect: Oscar Niemeyer
The long axis of the building runs east-west,
which makes sense in terms of the local climate.
The plinth storey is ventilated from beneath.
The main spaces are accessed externally, allowing
the offices to be cross-ventilated.

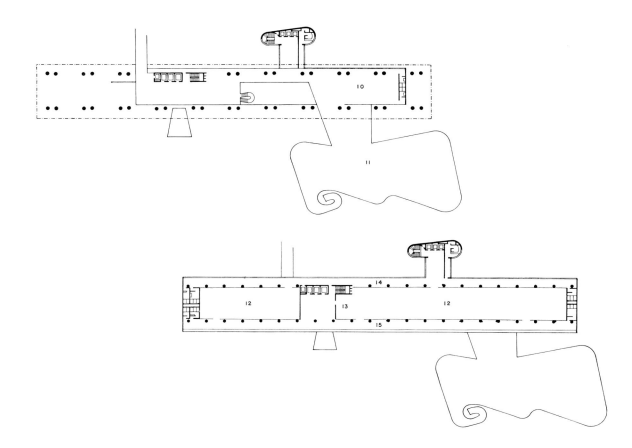

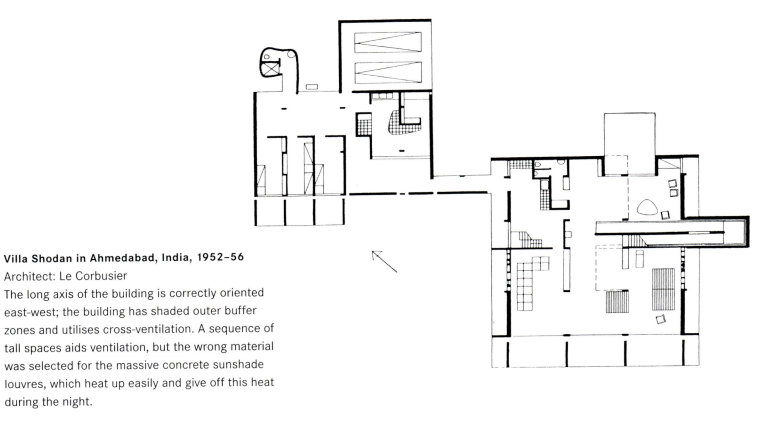

144   **Villa Shodan in Ahmedabad, India, 1952–56**
Architect: Le Corbusier
The long axis of the building is correctly oriented
east-west; the building has shaded outer buffer
zones and utilises cross-ventilation. A sequence of
tall spaces aids ventilation, but the wrong material
was selected for the massive concrete sunshade
louvres, which heat up easily and give off this heat
during the night.

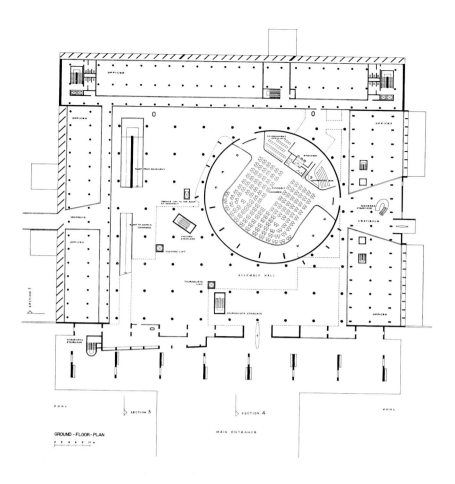

GROUND - FLOOR - PLAN

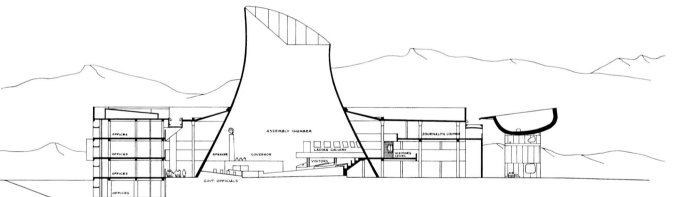

Buildings in the northern Indian savannah, 1956
Architect: Le Corbusier

The Parliament building in Chandigarh has an external buffer zone formed by the administration spaces and a protected reduit made up of the foyer and the parliament chamber. The tall parliament chamber is ventilated by a thermal (chimney) effect. The buildings are sensibly positioned with their long axes running east-west and can be cross-ventilated. However, ecological aspects were not taken into account in selecting the building materials (concrete, steel and

glass). These materials heat up excessively during the day and radiate the warmth they have stored until late into the night. Also illustrated here is the protected internal position ('reduit') of the parliament chamber and the foyer.

A climatically responsive concept is indicated by the opening up of the building on the freely-planned ground floor, as well as façades that can benefit from morning winds from the coast and the evening breezes from the land side. The projecting roof that is ventilated from below shades the façade against the steep rays of the northern sun (southern hemisphere).

Contributions by contemporary architects to a climatically responsive architecture

Australian architecture

Architect: Glenn Murcutt

This architect's buildings are characterised by an investigation of the topography of the site, the needs of the users and the climatic conditions. In the precise constructional details, the transparent spaces, the lightness of his architecture and its emphasis on functionality, the influence of classic modernism of, say, Mies van der Rohe, is clearly discernible.

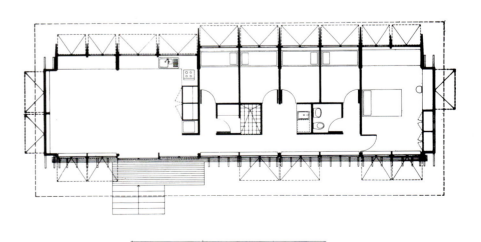

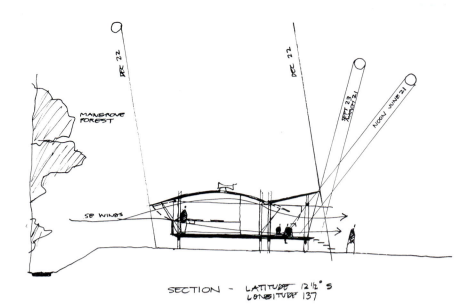

SECTION – LATITUDE 12½° S
LONGITUDE 137

Marika Alderton House, Northern Territory, Australia, 1991–94

Architect: Glenn Murcutt

This contribution to ecologically correct building in a hot and humid climatic zone is made by borrowing aspects of traditional architecture: the east-west placing of the building, the open timber-frame construction – a lightweight system that ensures limited heating up of the individual elements, an elevated plinth ventilated from below, cross-ventilation of the interior, light, unfolding sunshade elements and a projecting roof to protect against the rain.

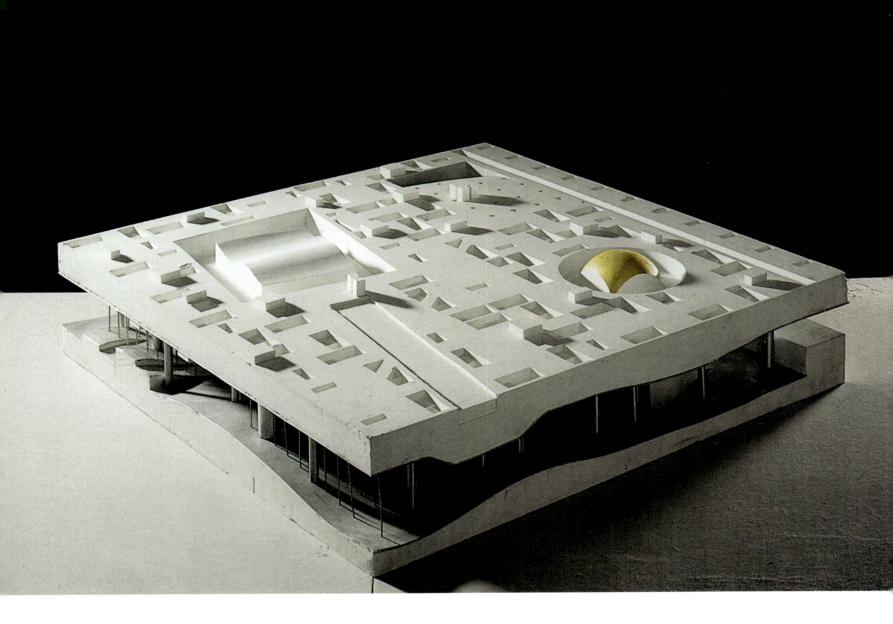

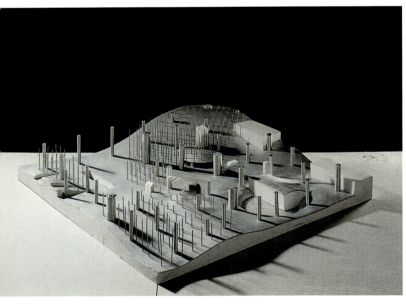

Models showing the roof of the hotel (top left), the urban space (bottom left) between the rooftop element and the plinth containing the conference centre, and a view of the sea (bottom right).

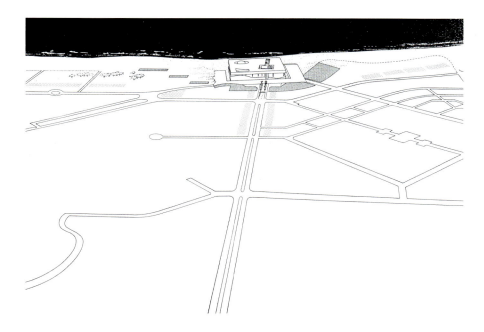

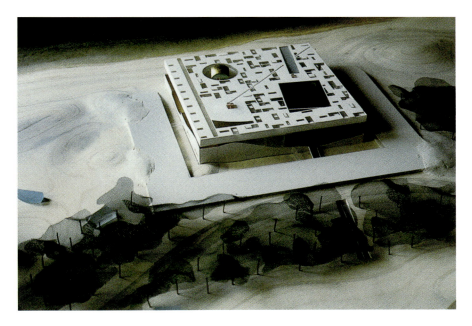

Congress centre and hotel in Agadir, Morocco, competition project, 1990
Architect: Rem Koolhaas / OMA
Location: on the southern periphery of Agadir in a eucalyptus wood on the Atlantic coast

The extensive schedule of accommodation includes a congress centre with its own hotel. The striking, quadratic, free-standing building is separated into a plinth and a roof element between which a beautiful urban space is created as a sheltered, sculpturally moulded area that refers to the nearby sea and surrounding sand dunes.
The imaginatively designed hotel is located in the roof element, its diverse guest suites facing onto internal courtyards with small turrets that offer guests a view of the sea.
The undulating roof to the plinth housing the conference centre forms an urban space that is orientated towards the landscape of the nearby beaches.
The concept of the project indicates an intelligent interpretation and development of traditional North African and Islamic building forms. The climatically appropriate design of the building and its sequence of spaces are particularly impressive.

150 **Cultural centre in Nouméa, New Caledonia, 1998**
Architect: Renzo Piano
These structures represent the most recent
approaches to climatically appropriate building
in the Tropics.
In the late 1990s, only a few architects demonstrated in their buildings that new approaches to a
climatically appropriate and ecological architecture
could be found by adopting traditional principles.

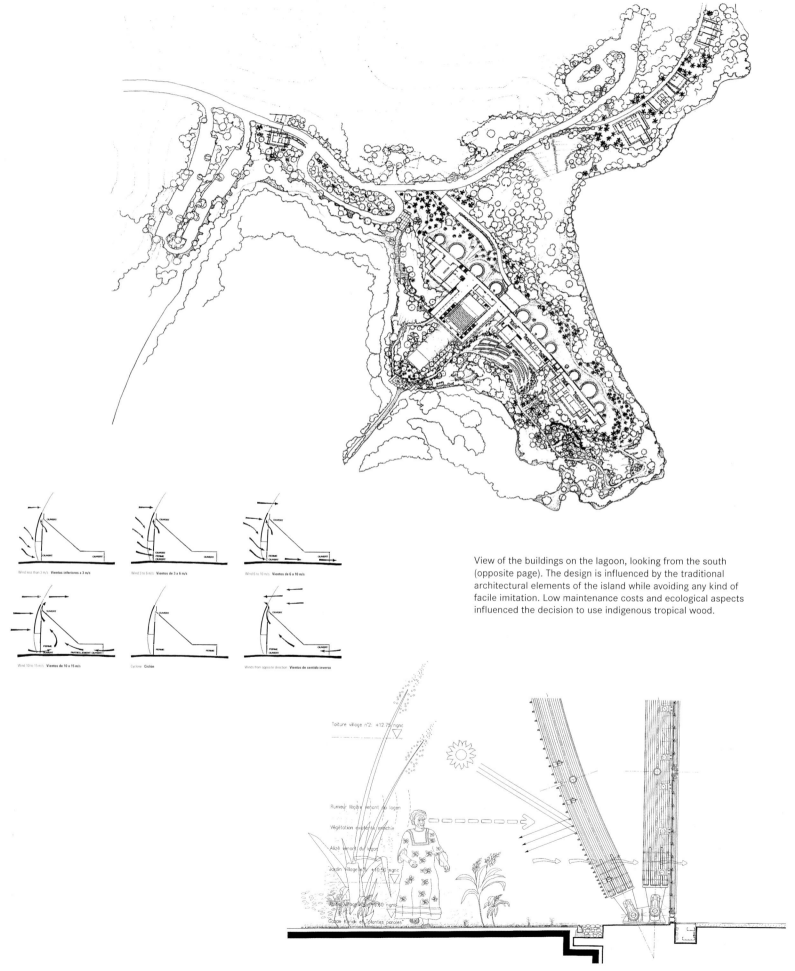

Wind less than 3 m/s **Vientos inferiores a 3 m/s**

Wind 3 to 6 m/s **Vientos de 3 a 6 m/s**

Wind 6 to 10 m/s **Vientos de 6 a 10 m/s**

Wind 10 to 15 m/s **Vientos de 10 a 15 m/s**

Cyclone **Ciclón**

Winds from opposite direction **Vientos de sentido inverso**

View of the buildings on the lagoon, looking from the south (opposite page). The design is influenced by the traditional architectural elements of the island while avoiding any kind of facile imitation. Low maintenance costs and ecological aspects influenced the decision to use indigenous tropical wood.

New contributions by the universities

University of Applied Sciences Constance
Institute for Applied Research
Wolfgang Lauber

These selected student designs were made after
the students had absolved preparatory seminars
on climatically appropriate building in the Tropics.
After having examined theoretical aspects of the
theme, the designs were then produced in the
creative phase, paying particular attention to the
ecological practicalities involved in using regional
building materials and employing local unskilled
workers.
Subsequently, during terms spent in the tropical
zones of Brazil and Africa, and in an application of
the 'learning by doing' principle, a number of buildings were built jointly by German students and local
students from the partner universities and with the
help of the future residents.

German Embassy in Accra, Ghana, 1996
Degree thesis: Sandra Bauer
University of Applied Sciences Constance

Building in a hot and humid climate: open architecture, with a large translucent roof made of per-
forated aluminium metal elements to provide shade.
The building opens to the south and the north, and
cross-ventilation is achieved by staggering the
individual elements.

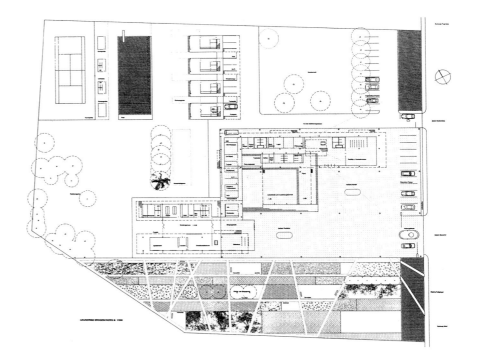

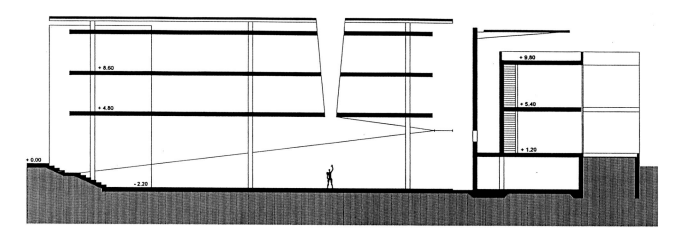

+ 8.60
+ 4.80
+ 0.00
− 2.20
+ 9.80
+ 5.40
+ 1.20

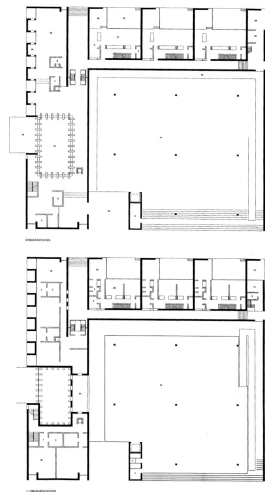

ERDGESCHOSS

I. OBERGESCHOSS

German Embassy in Accra, Ghana, 1996
Degree thesis: Daniele Dalla Corte
University of Applied Sciences Constance

Building in a hot and humid climate: compact, closed architecture
"The floor plan of a building should be as easy to read as a harmonious entity of spaces in light.
In fact, even a space that is supposed to be dark should receive at least enough light from a hidden opening so that one knows how dark it is inside."
(Louis I. Kahn)
Construction is designing with light. Walls are constructions that create a particular kind of light. Natural light enters the space from above and across the walls and is reflected by an area of water at the hall level. According to the position of the sun in the sky, the character and atmosphere of the individual areas of the rooms change. Through nuances the observer is made aware of the time of day. A roof light is used to light the central space of the chancellery. The light comes from the highest point, from the zenith, where it is strongest. Prism glasses are set in the sides of a wedge-shaped light shaft that penetrates all the levels of the chancellery and serve to deflect daylight into the neighbouring spaces. The light shaft is open to the sky.

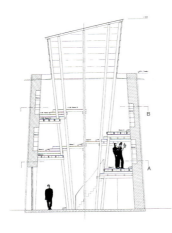

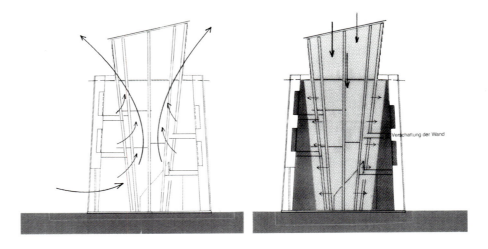

154 **Library tower for a vocational school in Rio de Janeiro, design: 1997**
Student group from the University of Applied Sciences Constance (Alexandra Mebus)

Building in a hot and humid climate
Construction: the solid walls are built of masonry and the bookshelves are integrated in them for climatic reasons. The masonry creates a stable, climatically-balanced environment in which the books can be safely stored.
Ventilation: as the doors of the library can be left open during the day, the roof light creates a 'chimney effect'. Cool air flowing close to ground level rises as it grows warmer and is conducted out of the building through glazing at the sides of the roof light. Light from the roof light can penetrate to the deepest zones of the space.

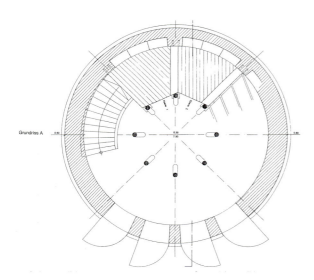

Illustrated at the top is the lighting and ventilation scheme.
The building is completed with water-resistant plywood panels.

Children's village near Rio de Janeiro

A further project in Brazil was the design of a children's village in Tangua, to the east of Rio de Janeiro, in collaboration with the PUC University in Rio de Janeiro. A dwelling house was planned as a pilot project and was built by a student group in the winter term of 1999. A most important aspect of this project was the use of the sustainable material wood – in the country with the richest timber resources in the world – instead of steel, cement and brick, which require large amounts of primary energy for their production.

In terms of building typology, the traditional principles of the 'building within a building' – the continuous shaded veranda running along the outside, cross-ventilation of the spaces through the entrances off the veranda and the raised floor slab ventilated from beneath – were all employed here. The two-storey building was built using a timber-frame structure with prefabricated frames made of solid timber uprights and double beams and was erected in only three weeks.

The frame building stands on raised footings on a prefabricated hollow element slab that is carried on strip foundations, which allows it to be ventilated from below, and also keeps it dry during the heavy tropical rainfall in this coastal region.

The roof covering is of tiles with an underlay and is ventilated from below. The buffer zone of the roof space (attic) is formed by an insulating suspended ceiling to the bedrooms on the upper floor.

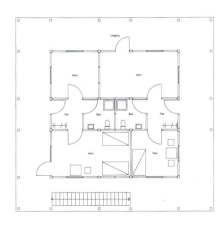
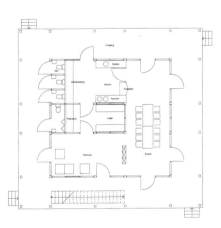

The building after the completion of the basic structure (top left) alongside the working model. The image on the left shows the prefabricated hollow-element slab.

A model of the cultural centre with the roof removed (bottom)
and plans of the ground and first floor (right)

156   **Cultural centre in the dry and hot climate**
of the savannah in Mali, 2000
Design: Gisela Gretschmann

A climatically appropriate solution that adopts the
traditional courtyard building principle was provided
by students from the University of Applied Sciences
Constance in their designs for their study project
2000. The real project for a cultural centre in Dogon
country, in Mali, allowed a contribution to be made
to the discussion about an architecture that offers
the new functions of an open cultural centre, set in
a traditional cultural landscape.
The building is for the most part closed to the public
street space; only the forecourt opens invitingly to
receive visitors and staff. The protected spaces for
the exhibition and staff are arranged around an inner
courtyard with shaded verandas.

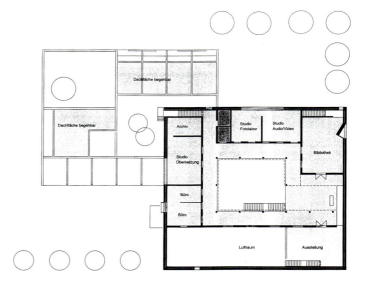

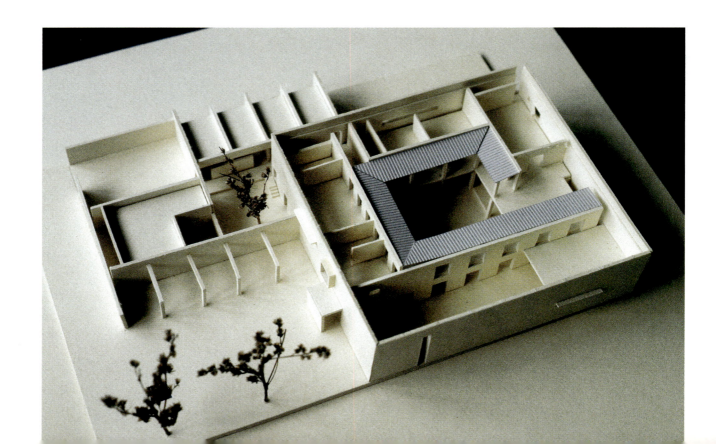

A small museum in Dogon country, Mali, 2004
Design: Wolfgang Lauber, planning: Neubauer, Grune, Göckeritz, Lenz

A second building project in the climatic zone of the savannah was carried out as part of a partnership project between the University of Constance and the E.N.I. University of Bamako and applied the educational principle of 'learning by doing'.

To integrate the building into the traditional cultural landscape it was built using a double shell of solid walls with exposed stonework (local sandstone) externally and an internal insulating layer of clay brickwork. Flat roofs were made in the traditional clay construction method with additional membrane layers to provide effective rain-proofing and with projecting waterspouts to divert the rainwater outwards. All these features helped to integrate the building into the traditional surroundings.

In a reference to traditional Dogon architecture, as shown in the floor plan (bottom left), the museum has a protected 'reduit' internal space for the exhibition, with surrounding buffer spaces providing thermal insulation which, in turn, are cross-ventilated in a north-south direction. The exhibition space is lit through high-level glazing that also provides cross-ventilation.

The building is closed to the east against the prevailing sand-bearing Harmattan wind and also against the low morning and evening sun. This reduces the extent to which the main spaces heat up. The veranda that opens to the south and is covered with a grass roof also helps in this respect.

Roof construction:
Structural round-section timber beams made of wood from the Ronier palm, which is resistant to termites. Above the beams is a layer of rods in the transverse direction made of split Ronier timbers with a clay layer, reinforced with wood shavings, and, on top, a reinforced waterproof insulating membrane.

Floor construction:
Sandstone slabs on compressed earth, cement-saving stone-laying system with smooth concrete screed
50/50-cm strip foundations made of rubble stone

Wall construction:
Externally: hand-cut, exposed sandstone masonry
Internally: a lining wall of clay bricks for better thermal insulation

The flat roof with clay screed and protective tiles on a waterproof membrane is drained by means of waterspouts that penetrate the parapet of the flat roof.

Traditional Dogon architecture used as a model (below)

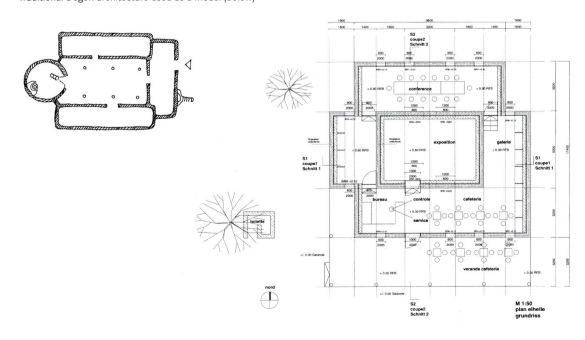

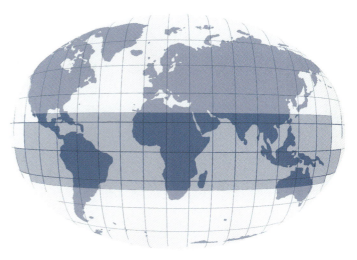

Urban Planning in Latin America, Africa and Asia

Population growth and a shortage of land has driven the apartment towers of Hong Kong to incredible heights.

Urban Panning in Rio de Janeiro, Brazil
Eckhart Ribbeck

Brazilian cities: high-rise buildings and tower apartment blocks as far as the eye can see. Urban density and property speculation have produced housing forms scarcely imaginable in European cities: Brazil's middle and upper classes live in dense developments of multi-storey apartment blocks and skyscrapers, the poor in improvised 'single-family houses' in favelas, or in the spontaneous developments on the periphery. Naturally, this kind of building is determined by socio-economic conditions, which in Latin America are more unequal than elsewhere.
In Rio de Janeiro, the genesis of these extremely diverse housing types can be traced in an almost exemplary fashion. The path taken by the development of housing for the wealthy or the bourgeoisie leads from the Portuguese colonial town to the European block that shaped the image of the city until the mid-20th century. After this time the 'American high-rise block' began increasingly to exert its influence, although less in the form of office towers and more as high-rise apartment buildings. Although this is at variance with both the European and the North American housing ideal, today, living in multi-storey apartment blocks or luxury tower blocks is one of the characteristics of the Brazilian megacities, as the skyline of São Paolo dramatically illustrates.
In the new urban development area of Barra da Tijuca, the 'Beach of the Towers', this development has arrived at a certain endpoint, as the process of separating the rich from the poor has been completed. At the same time, the advantages of the apartment tower have been consistently optimised. In an unspoiled, green environment where services are readily available and where there is, above all, a promise of security, the chaos of the metropolis is, so to speak, eliminated. At the same time, the extreme density demanded by the speculative property market is achieved. Unimpressed by local traditions and European urban models the metropolis is now producing artificial districts, luxury ghettos and gated communities – a kind of post-European urban planning that pragmatically bears the consequences of the weakness of official planning bodies, property speculation, poverty and the feeling of lack of safety.

Densification and 'Copacabanisation'
Before 1900, the coast had little importance as a place to live. On the contrary, the noisy, dirty port, the warehouses, fishers and smugglers meant that early developments near the coast, in fact, turned their back on the sea. It was only at the turn of the century that elegant sea-baths and promenades came into fashion and living by the sea became the main motor of an urban development that, up to the present day, has steamrolled any topographical, economic or planning resistance.
As early as the 1920s and '30s, the small beach houses in the Gloria, Flamengo and Botafogo districts began to disappear and were replaced by apartment buildings and hotels. Copacabana was opened up in 1885 by the construction of a tunnel. With the Avenida Atlantica (1919) the development became more intensive, but in the 1930s Copacabana was still a district of villas and summer houses. Around 1950 Copacabana advanced to an international seaside resort and an exclusive district, the villas disappeared and were replaced by 10-storey apartment blocks that still dominate the district to this day. The external increase in density was followed by an internal one – a phenomenon also known as 'Copacabanisation'. The large, expensive apartments were subdivided and the population density increased to 1,000 inhabitants per hectare. The pressure exerted by traffic and commercialisation followed so that by the end of the 1970s the elegant image was already more than slightly tarnished.

Today, Copacabana is dominated by a milieu that gives the district a lively character; Art Deco and early Modernist buildings contribute to the charm of the area with their elegantly curved façades and horizontal bands of glazing. A particularly fine example is Oscar Niemeyer's atelier building on Avenida Atlantica. At the same time, many features are at variance with the normal concept of a good middle- and upper-class residential area, above all, the proximity of the favelas, whose inhabitants naturally use the jobs and infrastructure offered by Copacabana. The two inner main roads are busy traffic thoroughfares with a constant stream of cars and buses. Nevertheless, the rents are high, whereby the price of an apartment is directly related to its closeness to the sea. There are around 40 flats in a typical apartment building, most of them in the form of rented accommodation.

In the densely developed urban district there are hardly any open or green spaces. This lends the beach a particular significance: it offers views, air and sun, and is an area for relaxation and sport, a boulevard and a central park. The beach provides a setting for huge beach parties and concerts, and on fine weekends it is filled by several hundred thousand people, many of them from the poor outer suburbs. At other times it is almost empty and belongs to the children from the favela, the fishers and the macumba groups that celebrate their rituals here. Avenida Atlantica is both an overcrowded motorway and an elegant strand boulevard which, when closed to traffic at weekends, transforms into a twenty-kilometre-long promenade, leisure and sports area. In the hot and humid Tropics, the European block is not ideal, as it does not allow cross-ventilation and only the front of the building facing the beach profits from the sea breezes. The pilotis, the columns that elevate the first floor, allow some air to enter the narrow backyards, while vegetation in the front gardens and on the streets also provides some shade and coolness. In earlier times, high rooms, large, cross-ventilated apartments and ceiling ventilators helped to make the indoor climate bearable. In the course of the increase in density these qualities were gradually lost, the ground-floor areas and courtyards were built over and in the smaller, subdivided apartments there is little possibility of cross-ventilation. This explains why hundreds of air-conditioning appliances that simply devour energy are mounted on the façades and in the windows; in the hot months they are essential for a certain degree of domestic comfort.

Despite the problems and the obvious overcrowding there is still a relaxed air in Copacabana that gives the district a certain appeal and a domestic feeling. Occasionally, one still finds the small-scale structure of a district that has developed gradually and there is even room in the narrow streets for weekly markets. However, today, Copacabana lives largely on its capital, and it is impossible to overlook its age. Through-traffic, beach life and large events place this district under considerable pressure, which is why real estate agents have long since directed their attention to other areas.

With the urban development project Rio Cidade, which effectively renewed both the Avenida Atlantica and the main roads, the municipal authorities sought to combat the decline of the area. There is also a new underground station, which has somewhat reduced the enormous volume of bus traffic. On the other hand, the underground line means that the pressure of densification and change will further increase, and only strict planning and building controls can prevent the old apartment buildings from gradually vanishing and being replaced by new, taller apartment houses and tower blocks.

From block to tower

Ipanema und Leblon, the smarter residential districts of Rio, lie on a narrow tongue of land bordered by the sea and the Rodrigues de Freitas

Luxury Apartment with views of the sea as well as traffic congestion are typical characteristics on the few main roads of the wealthy districts in the Zona Sul.

lagoon. In the 1930s, Ipanema was also a loose development of villas and summer houses. In the 1940s, however, the first wave of densification began, leading to the development of four-storey blocks. Because of speculative property prices this modest level of development did not survive long and since then 15- to 20-storey buildings have sprouted out of the ground throughout the district. The skyline of Ipanema is therefore not homogeneous and compact, as it is in Copacabana, but is characterised by the differences in the height of buildings, the building lines and the street spaces. The changing building regulations have had an effect in this respect: for every metre that a building was set back further from the street an extra storey could be added; equally, the ground floors can often be used as garages and the buildings made accordingly higher.

Like in Copacabana, the main street is an overcrowded traffic artery, but the traffic situation is somewhat better as the shore roads running along the lagoon take the through-traffic to São Conrado and Barra da Tijuca. The renovation of the lagoon has turned its shoreline into an expensive development area and the proximity to the elegant clubs and to the Botanical Gardens enhances its attractiveness.

As a whole, Ipanema is less densely developed than Copacabana; despite the tall apartment buildings one can still find many quiet and green residential streets. In a tropical climate, free-standing tower developments offer clear advantages over closed European-style development. This applies not only to the individual apartments but also to the entire district, as the ventilation in a district made up of towers is considerably better.

If they are well located, the slender towers (often with only one or two apartments per floor) have a view of the sea and in the hot and humid Tropics they represent an almost ideal building form. However, the potential for natural air-conditioning is hardly exploited at all because air-conditioning is taken for granted and, therefore, climatically appropriate building plays only a minor role.

The population density in Ipanema is still considerable lower and the social profile more exclusive than in Copacabana. This also applies to the beach, which is largely reserved for the better-off classes. However, the numerous building sites indicate that in both Ipanema and Leblon densification is moving ahead. The lower buildings that have survived from the 1940s and '50s are disappearing more and more,

and smaller sites are being combined to provide space for new housing towers.

Today, the beach, the lagoon and a number of open spaces and parks still ensure that the process of 'Copacabanisation' is kept in check. This area is at the highpoint of its attractiveness and can certainly preserve this level for a decade or two. At the same time, a huge rival district being created in Barra da Tijuca will challenge Ipanema's position as the most desirable residential area.

From the tower to the luxury ghetto

The most important expansion area in the southern zone is Barra da Tijuca. In addition to an almost untouched 20-kilometre-long beach this enormous development area has a number of lagoons and an extensive hinterland, which includes the town of Jacarapaguá. The oldest development area is Jardim Oceánico, a modern garden city with three-storey apartment blocks. Towards the south the form of the buildings changes dramatically: a forest of 30-storey tower blocks announces that this is where the suburban idyll ends and that henceforth a completely different scale applies.

The plan to develop this beach and lagoon area, which was once a protected nature reservation, was formulated at the end of the 1960s. Lucio Costa planned a 15-kilometre-long ribbon town called 'Novo Rio'. To avoid completely ruining the lagoon landscape, Costa proposed a 'Beach of Towers' – loosely distributed groups of tower blocks placed along the express highways. Like in Brasilia, the centre is formed by a highway interchange that is surrounded by huge shopping centres and open spaces. Here, however, instead of leading to a district of government buildings, as in Brasilia, the east-west axis leads to the future Centro Metropolitano of monumental dimensions, which could accommodate the entire old centre of Rio de Janeiro. This huge reserve area is, however, only partly developed and serves at present more as a protective cordon sanitaire against the poor neighbouring town of Jacarapaguá. The dimensions of the planned centre clearly show that Barra da Tijuca will not be a normal suburb but a large new urban zone which, in the long term, will offer room for half a million inhabitants.

The proximity of completed and incomplete districts is also reminiscent of Brasilia, as are the vast deserts of car park spaces in front of the temples of commerce, and the masses of workers and employees that alight from innumerable buses every

Once planned by Lucio Costa and Oscar Niemeyer as the "Beach of Towers", Barra da Tijuca is now the most important area in development in Rio de Janeiro.

According to the standard regulations, the private developments have a right to public schools but they prefer to erect private kindergartens and primary schools in order to control admission.

Naturally, the gated communities are surrounded by walls and the entrances are guarded by security staff. Having passed through the gate one enters a service area where the administration, shops and taxi ranks are located. This is the contact point for visitors, suppliers, craftsmen and domestic staff, who are required in large numbers to run this luxury ghetto. Inside the development the need for security has almost reached the level of an obsession. Private police patrol the streets and the villas are surrounded by walls and protected by alarms and guard dogs. The peace of the green residential streets is only occasionally disturbed by expensive cars; the few people on foot are generally domestic staff, guards or joggers.

The luxury islands are equipped with leisure clubs, sports and play areas, swimming pools and small private parks. Fitness centres are a part of the typical Rio body cult, as everyone wants to look their best on the beach. Several of the *condominios fechados* have landing stages on the lagoons, from where one can travel by private boat to the open sea. The level of service goes far beyond the traditional porter, security guard and maid found in every apartment building. Not only the individual building but the entire district is a specialist residential business. In the expensive Apart-Hotels there is a comprehensive flat service. Obviously, there exists a well-off clientele whose mobile lifestyle demands a hotel-like way of living.

The luxury *condominios fechados* offer security, comfort and recreation like exclusive holiday clubs but, of course, all of this has to be paid for. As the service charges often exceed 500 euros, in many of the new private communities the range of facilities has been somewhat reduced.

morning. But the classic six-storey housing blocks of the Superquadras in Brasilia are hardly to be found at all in Barra da Tijuca. The speculative use of land ensured a high building density and the construction of housing towers here from the very start. The introverted neighbourhoods generally consist of a group of towers around which luxurious communal facilities and small areas of villas are arranged. Elegant names emphasise the exclusive nature of these gated communities: Riviera Club, Village Oceanique, Nova Ipanema. Only a Nova Copacabana is lacking, as this ageing district is no longer seen as having any advertising value.

In Barra da Tijuca urban planning is developing to an extreme a number of tendencies that are also to be found in Ipanema: the classic apartment building becomes an introverted private housing development; with hotel-like services and facilities they have something of the quality of a hotel; and the building height increases to 30 storeys. The privatisation of entire neighbourhoods does not comply with current legislation, which requires that at least the streets remain public, but this is obviously not observed.

Barra da Tijuca – the up to 30 storey-high apartment towers of this "luxury ghetto" feature every imaginable service including private sports facilities, recreational clubs and childcare facilities.

Barra da Tijuca is an important source of employment, even though most of the jobs are badly paid. If one adds up the domestic staff, security guards, building workers and the staff in the large shopping centres, this explains the uninterrupted stream of buses travelling in the direction of Barra da Tijuca. The fact that thousands of people who work in Barra come from the poor areas and the favelas represents a security risk for the rich districts that cannot be eliminated by walls and gates.

Gigantic shopping centres complete the range of facilities offered, the most important being Barra Shopping, Latin America's largest shopping mall. This introverted large container rising above an enormous wasteland of car parking spaces has kilometres of shopping arcades on several levels. In addition to shops, there are also cinemas, restaurants, gaming halls and Sunday concerts. Air-conditioning, luxury and security are taken for granted, which makes Barra Shopping popular with families and young people from the entire Zona Sul.

Condominios fechados and shopping are the two poles around which everyday life in Barra da Tijuca revolves. Some private developments run their own small buses that travel back and forth between the apartment blocks and the shopping centre. The kind of urban openness that is to be found in traditional cities does not exist in Barra da Tijuca. This is compensated for by the social life in the leisure and sports clubs and there are also a number of citizens' associations that are deeply involved in the further

development of the new town. But, naturally, the perfect stage for self-presentation and communication is – like in Copacabana and Ipanema – the beach, which on fine weekends attracts the *cariocas* in masses. In the surroundings there are numerous restaurants, cinemas and hotels, which is why a part of Rio de Janeiro's leisure scene has moved to this new urban district.

Barra da Tijuca gives the middle and upper classes what the chaos of the metropolis took away from them: security, comfort and a relatively intact environment. But, of course, the new city does not have what old Rio possesses in abundance: history, identity and public life. The rigorous separation of rich and poor that has been carried out to a considerable degree in Barra da Tijuca is a point wide open to criticism. But Barra da Tijuca is a young city, and therefore the growth of population and density will also bring with it changes to the character of the streets and the public spaces. This is already discernible, for example, in the central motorway that is changing rapidly into a commercial corridor densely lined by office blocks and commercial buildings. Even the gated communities could open up once again if safety can be ensured – as is shown by a number of new projects that are less rigorously closed off. And so the final word about Barra da Tijuca has certainly not been spoken. Like every Latin American city, Novo Rio is also subject to a dynamic process of change, so that no one can say with certainty how it will look in 20 years' time.

Mexico City

Informal Modernism – Spontaneous Building in Mexico City

Like in other megacities, the spectrum of housing types in Mexico City is extremely broad. While the luxury of the rich districts reaches an almost provocative level, the poor districts lack even the most basic amenities. At the same time, new housing and building typologies are developing that differ clearly from European models. This applies to the gated communities that are being created on the periphery as well as to the spontaneous or informal settlements of the poor urban population, which is largely excluded from the formal land and housing market. The massive phenomenon of self-build housing shows that even in the megacities the vernacular tradition of building one's own house with one's own hands is experiencing a major renaissance, rather than dying out – albeit under completely different circumstances to the traditional or rural context.

The chaotic 'invasions' of earlier years have resulted in an irregular property market that organises the housing for the poor in a profit-oriented way. Throughout the periphery irregular land speculators and property dealers subdivide the land into small lots and sell these to low-income families, who erect their precarious self-build houses there. Usually, there is no urban infrastructure, which means that self-builders not only build their house with immense effort, but also construct streets, water supply and other facilities to make the land habitable. At the same time, the informal settlers have to battle against the threats and discrimination that they are subjected to from the municipal authorities and the well-off urban population.

For decades, urban policies and planning have been incapable of offering a housing alternative to the poor, and so irregular settling and building have become a sort of 'safety valve' for the social pressure

created by the lack of land and housing. The attitude of politicians and planners is accordingly ambivalent: on the one hand, the spontaneous settlements threaten the prevailing order, which implies a rigorous control and repression, while on the other hand, these settlements represent the only realistic solution for low-income families to gain access to a piece of land. In political terms, the alternating threats, indifference and support have proved to be an effective instrument in keeping the poor urban masses dependent and under control.

The recipe of the irregular land dealers is simple: a schematic land subdivision and freedom to build on the plot – these are the basic components of 'modern' spontaneous settlements. Moreover, the strict grid pattern of the informal settlements fits well into the 500-year-old chequerboard tradition of Hispano-America's cities. Also, the courtyard house which the poor families normally build is the heir to a long tradition that ranges from the *patios* of the Spaniards to the *calpullis* of the Aztecs.

The grid pattern makes the further development of informal settlements very flexible, so that over the years a precarious building site can develop into a consolidated urban area or even into a dense business and commercial district. Naturally, the limited means of the self-builders and their irregular status initially produce a poor housing area, but even at this stage every house is unique in terms of floor plan, size and decoration.

In the context of a megacity, spontaneous building is not only tied to tradition, but is also extremely adaptable as it is carried out by people who often work in the regular construction industry and who are therefore familiar with modern building methods. Everything they can afford and which has proved useful is assimilated in self-help building and for this reason the houses often show a hybrid character that is located somewhere between traditional, improvised and modern building. The same applies

to the house types, floor plans and façades, as well as to the construction, which is generally a minimal concrete frame filled with bricks or concrete blocks. Thus the self-build house can be extended step by step and in the course of time can transform from a precarious hut into a respectable town house. For poor families the house is the most important anchor in the metropolitan chaos: it must accommodate a rapidly growing family as well as productive or commercial activities in order to generate an income, for example, with a small shop, a workshop or by letting rooms. At the same time, the house must offer a safe retreat, where the family can survive in times of sickness or unemployment. When times are better, the house is extended and altered until it reaches a considerable size. The typical self-build house is therefore an extremely flexible shell that reacts to every change within the family and allows survival at a minimum standard as well as middle-class integration. This is in contrast to the conventional low-cost house, an optimised 'container' that can hardly be extended or altered at all, designed

to accommodate an average family and a particular income group. In such low-cost housing schemes, productive activities such as shops and workshops are often expressly forbidden in order to ensure a uniform and clean appearance.

In Mexico City, like in most other developing countries, it is not official projects that are the pacemakers in housing for the poor, but large-scale self-help building. This means that every planning concept fails if it does not take into account the experience of informal building. This is confirmed by innumerable low-cost housing projects which – while providing a small number of people with a roof over their heads – have shown hardly any large-scale effect, whereas the ubiquitous concrete columns of incomplete self-build houses have become a world-wide symbol of informal settlements. Informal building is, therefore, neither a traditional activity nor a helpless improvisation, but rather a tested strategy that – despite poverty and countless problems – is able to conquer gradually a piece of urban land and life.

After 20 or 30 years, many of the quarters of self-made dwellings are denser and more consolidated, however, there remain serious challenges to provide these areas with basic services.

"Huts become homes" as a result of expansion in districts of self-made dwellings; expansion which often leads to high construction and population densities

In Latin America there exists extensive literature on informal building, focussing mostly on the political, economic and social conditions, for example, the illegal occupation of land, the political confrontations and the precarious living standard. The older informal settlements, which make up almost half of Mexico City, are dealt with less because they are already more or less integrated and are viewed as less problematic. But even these settlements, many of them 40 or more years old, are left to themselves, as urban planning lacks goals, funds and instruments to steer informal housing on a large scale.

In many cases it is still unclear how informal settlements will develop in the long term. Will the process of urban consolidation, which has obviously occurred in the majority of cases, continue in the future? Or will the urban development break off at a certain point because the informal settlements have grown old, the infrastructure is overloaded and chaotic densification is taking place? In other words: does the development of informal settlements almost automatically lead to consolidated and integrated urban areas, or is it a cyclical phenomenon that in the long term will create new problem areas or even slums?

As informal settlements have existed in Mexico City for around half a century, the long-term results of self-building are perhaps more clear in this megacity then elsewhere. But in Mexico City, too, there is no uniform pattern of informal building but rather a broad spectrum that ranges from precarious slum areas to well-established residential and commercial districts, whose irregular origins are nowadays hardly discernible.

However, in the majority of cases some common characteristics can be found showing the potential and limits of self-building. About 60 per cent of the houses are traditional courtyard houses and 40 per cent are compact houses without a courtyard. Thus the traditional courtyard house still dominates, but

at the same time 'terraced houses' and hybrid house types are becoming more common, as small sites make the erection of courtyard houses more difficult and commercial activities demand another building typology. Furthermore, middle-class housing penetrates the informal settlements, also changing the housing typology.

After 30 years, around 30 per cent of the self-build houses are still single-storey, 50 per cent are two-storey and 20 per cent are three-storey. The upper floors are generally not completely developed; the third floor in particular is usually just a building site or a provisional roof. Completed three-storey houses often contain rented flats or business premises erected professionally and leased by small local investors.

The results of self-building are remarkable but not spectacular. On average, a new room is added to the house every three to five years, with a further storey added after ten to fifteen years. Many self-build houses hardly change any further after the first decade or two, as the needs of the family have been met and the economic and architectonic limits of self-building have been reached. Such saturated houses usually have two storeys and five to eight rooms, which offers enough space even for extended families. The 'ideal' house, which people try to build in many variations, would generally include a workshop or shop on the ground floor, living rooms upstairs, extensions for relatives or to let, a courtyard and roof terrace. Naturally, many poor families never reach this stage, whereas others manage to transform their house into a commercial property or apartment building.

The consolidation of informal settlements is inevitably hampered by limited income and lack of other resources. Thus the majority of them remains at the stage of 'semi-consolidated areas' with two-storey houses and many commercial activities, but also with a great number of unsolved problems and signs of stagnation. Even after 30 years many houses still lack finishing, the upper storey is still a building site, and many are already ageing visibly. Nevertheless, these semi-consolidated areas allow a more or less normal urban life, living conditions are poor but tolerable, the cost of living is relatively low and most basic services are available, albeit at a low level. This allows poorer families to survive, as well as giving better earners a chance to develop.

In this regard, the semi-consolidated settlements show a certain balance between income and built environment, between formality and informality, between order and improvisation. This is, of course, a volatile state that is constantly threatened by decline and detoriation, as well as by gentrification and expulsion of the poorest. Whether an informal settlement improves or declines depends upon a number of factors: the social characteristics of the inhabitants, the involvement of the municipal administration, and, above all, the metropolitan growth and change that brings with it advantages or disadvantages for a certain area.

Like the chaotic 'invasions' of three or four decades ago, the irregular land subdivisions are now encountering obstacles: the increasing shortage of urban land, stagnating incomes, rising building and transport costs, as well as stricter planning control all combine to slow down the growth of irregular settlements on the periphery. This has led to an 'urban implosion', which further intensifies the housing pressure on the core city. This is evident not only in Mexico City but also in other large Latin American cities which, after a phase of dramatic expanse, are now experiencing increasing density.

Most of the old informal settlements have been legalised after decades of uncertainty and are now relatively well integrated in the metropolis. They play an important role in the market for rented accommodation as well as for commercial activities. In this way, these settlements are transformed into dense urban areas where the usual limits of self-building are far exceeded. Increasing building heights and densities attract more commercial activities and inevitably push up land prices and rents, putting the remaining small family houses under pressure. This is particularly true when major urban projects, such as the construction of a new metro line or a commercial centre, are being carried out nearby. Strategically located settlements often take on the function of a commercial area with a mixed land use, where apartment buildings, shops and workshops increasingly replace the self-build family houses.

Of course, the long-term development of informal settlements takes place in a complex and contradictory way. A well-consolidated core zone can often be found alongside incomplete and precarious fringe areas. In many cases nobody can say for sure what direction the further development will take – an optimistic view is just as plausible as a pessimistic one that predicts increasing social and urban problems.

The founding of a spontaneous settlement on the outer periphery is always an uncertain undertaking. It takes on average a generation before an informal settlement is more or less consolidated and enjoys all the facilities that one expects in an urban context. However, most areas remain at a semi-consolidated stage, hampered by isolation and lack of infrastructure. The preconditions for further integration cannot be achieved until the dynamic growth of the metropolis has caught up with an informal settlement. By that stage the practices of self-building and low-tech urbanism no longer suffice: land use and building density must be controlled, the traffic regulated, the infrastructure developed. In addition, open space often is completely lacking in informal areas – acquires a particular importance. Also, the public space and architectural design must be cared for. All this demands a form of urban planning and public intervention that is usual in other established districts. Where this is the case, land and property prices rise, leading to an increasing conflict between the high value of the sites and

the old self-build houses standing on them. As a result, more and more houses are replaced by capital-intensive buildings and new urban functions – and informal building and urbanism, having served their purpose, can then leave the stage.

Even the appearance of the street is greatly improved by the decoration and design of the facades

Anonymous vernacular building in Africa and Brazil

Wolfgang Lauber

The vernacular architecture of the garden courtyard house

The open house in the planted and enclosed garden courtyard represents a suitable model for living in a tropical climate, a model that has been tried and tested in traditional rural areas over a lengthy period of time and today is being used once again in the urban suburbs (perimeter developments) of the megacities.

Its advantages lie in the separation of the private space for the family from the public street space, the possibility of erecting the house in a series of small steps to suit the financial possibilities of a young family, and the ease of adaptation to meet new requirements through horizontal expansion or the addition of a storey.

Compared with the expensive official architecture of urban housing programmes, anonymous self-build has a further advantage in that it uses simple building materials and, with the help of friends and family, allows dwellings to be built far more cheaply.

A number of examples from Africa – the rural region of northern Togo and the urban area of the large city of Lomé, in Togo – illustrate this concept.

In the northern savannah of Africa the traditional compounds are made up of a group of huts arranged in a circle inside a courtyard enclosed by a wall and planted with trees to provide shade. The entrance is traditionally from the west. The internal courtyard offers space for daily life and ensures that the nights retain their peace and quiet.

A variation on this courtyard type is the courtyard house in southern Ghana, where the rectangular individual houses are also arranged around a spacious courtyard. Only the main house has an entrance from the road; the other houses open onto the courtyard through an open veranda.

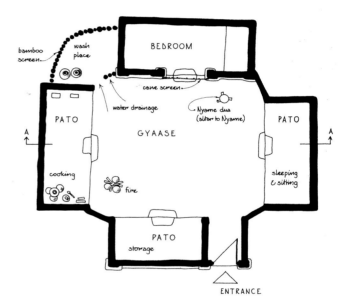

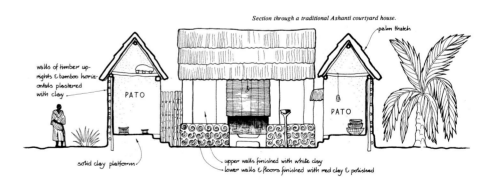

Compound of the Moba and Kotokoli in northern Togo (top)
Traditional forms of the garden courtyard house in rural areas of the African savannah as illustrated by a compound type in southern Ghana (centre and bottom)

A view inside a compound of the Dogon, Mali (opposite page)

Urban examples of a garden courtyard house
A new garden courtyard house (above) is constructed using the self-build system, employing cheap building materials and a simple structural concept and detailing.
Examples of planted domestic courtyards in the urban area of the savannah are shown above and bottom left.
The building materials chosen are often climatically inappropriate. Examples of this (top) illustrate an incorrect orientation towards the sun, a lack of shade towards the exterior walls, and insufficient insulation of the exterior walls through the use of solid sand-and-cement blocks or concrete surfaces.

An urban concept in the coastal city of Lomé, Togo: continuous greenery (top) open to the ventilating sea breezes, and private areas in garden courtyards on a public street (bottom)

Building without an external drainage system or other measures against rising damp leads to severe dampness in the interior and thus to wet rot (right). This frequently causes allergies and asthma-related illnesses among the inhabitants.

Site plan (opposite page, top) of the 'Sitio de Ferro' favela in Niterói and a floor plan of house type 1 favoured by the favela dwellers: c. 20 m², with a dry toilet and a rainwater cistern.

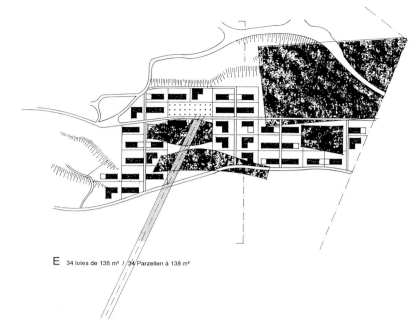

E 34 lotes de 138 m² / 34 Parzellen à 138 m²

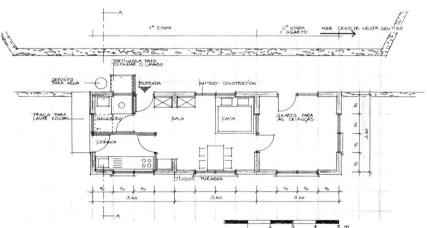

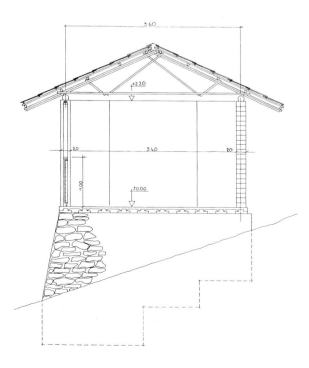

Housing construction in a favela in Rio de Janeiro, Brazil

Favelas, the informally erected housing developments of the poor on the periphery of the large cities in Brazil, seldom have an adequate infrastructure. Neither ownership of the site nor the buildings themselves are legally approved. In Rio, the topography in conjunction with the local climate creates a serious problem, as a large number of the favelas are located on steep slopes in the hilly peripheral districts of the city. The clearing of the sites has led to severe erosion of the unprotected ground during heavy rainfall. The sites often offer poor building ground and have such steep slopes that the heavy rainfall threatens the stability of the houses and can even cause them to collapse by undermining them. The consequences to date have included entire developments sliding down the hillside.

In the context of a joint research study between the University of Applied Sciences Constance and the Architecture Faculty of the Universidade Federal Fluminense (NEPHU Institute) in Niterói, Rio de Janeiro, a new, more economic house type was developed and built as a prototype in the favela 'Sitio de Ferro' in Niterói.

During the concept phase, around 20 students from the University of Applied Sciences Constance devoted a number of seminars to investigating the urban, architectural and construction aspects of the surroundings of the favela in Niterói. As a preparatory measure three students spent some time in Rio de Janeiro in 1995.

The NEPHU Institute had already worked in close collaboration with residents in a number of favelas in Niterói over a period of several years and had gained their trust during this time. The favela residents showed great willingness to collaborate on this project. They expected the development of a prototype dwelling house that would suit their needs (as well as their financial capacity) and one that they

could build largely by themselves. In this context, self-build is the usual method of providing housing: the expectations made of this project therefore included achieving the most favourable possible balance between low material costs, short construction period, stability on site and permanence.

The standard construction of the favela houses
During the period immediately following the move to the city the typology of the houses in the favelas was still shaped by the rural origins of the residents. Traditional construction methods, such as taipa or adobe construction, were gradually replaced under the influence of the dominant urban images. The aim was to copy the houses in which the well-off middle and upper classes lived, albeit at a far smaller scale. These houses were solid stuccoed buildings with concrete floor slabs, heavy timber roof structures and roof tiles. Ecologically and economically more sensible approaches generally met with little acceptance, especially if they looked like 'mud and bamboo huts' and were rejected as not being 'up to date'. Consequently, the small favela houses are generally built in a solid mixed construction system, whereby, due to a shortage of funds, savings are made – generally at the wrong places – in order to be able to afford senseless prestigious elements. The walls made of hollow blocks or brickwork are generally only 10 centimetres thick and are strengthened by concrete corner piers. The roof construction, made of cut, rot-resistant tropical hardwood, rests directly on the walls, frequently without a wall plate to transfer the load. In most cases the roof is covered with corrugated asbestos cement sheeting or tiles. The floors of multi-storey buildings are made of in-situ concrete or hollow-element systems. The doors and windows are usually expensive prefabricated wood or steel elements.

Often, at the start of developing a sloping site, the existing growth of bamboo is felled, which leads rapidly to the loss of the thin top layer of topsoil. The remaining earth is then formed into terraces. The walls are not given foundations but are placed directly on the wet ground. This means that, during heavy rainfall, water often washes under the load-bearing external walls, increasing the danger of the buildings collapsing.
Wells serve as the source of water but are frequently polluted by wastewater that flows unfiltered across the site, some of it inevitably seeping into the ground. The residents occasionally build cisterns of corrugated asbestos cement or use metal barrels to collect the rainwater from the roofs to supply the kitchens and bathrooms.
In August 1996, the students and teachers from Constance presented their project 'Dwelling House for the Favelas' to the municipal administration in Rio-Niterói, as well as to the future residents. After working out, improving and completing the design jointly, work began on building a prototype together.
The favela house is based on a 90-centimetre grid that generates axis centres of 3.60 metres. Prefabricated units, in particular doors and window frames of bamboo, reduce the construction time and simplify the self-build process. The building costs can be considerably reduced by the appropriate choice of materials. The following is a description of the construction of this prototype:
► The house is not cut into the slope but stands on strip foundations that are adapted to the individual outline of each particular slope by stepping them. The strip foundations are built parallel to the slope and inserted so deep into the earth that they stand on dry ground and project about 50 cm above ground level. The floor slab lies on these foundations at an adequate distance from the ground so that rainwater can run off under the house. Thus no obstruction is offered to the considerable amounts of rainwater and the floor slab remains dry. The strip foundations are very economical thanks to the use of 'rock concrete'. To produce this material, crudely cut stones are stacked in an improvised formwork and the voids around and between the stones are filled with cement mortar – without the use of reinforcement.

The dry substructure (opposite page): an elevated floor slab made of prefabricated hollow brick elements (left) and building the 20-centimetre-thick brickwork corners that stiffen the walls (right).

► A prefabricated hollow block floor slab is laid above the strip foundations, at a height of about 50 cm.

► For the exterior walls, 'T' or L-shaped load-bearing sections are built using 20-centimetre-thick brickwork. This is a simple way of stiffening the exterior walls and makes the expensive concrete corners generally used unnecessary. Prefabricated walls made of bamboo and wood are placed in the openings between these solid elements. For the non-load-bearing walls, such as parapets 10 centimetres thick, walls built of hollow bricks are adequate.

► Roof construction:

A wall plate made from a round timber section lies on the load-bearing wall elements. It is anchored to the corners by iron bolts to transfer wind loads. The dimensions of the roof trusses are calculated by a structural engineer (in order to avoid the standard oversizing of such elements) and are made of economical bamboo cane to reduce both weight and costs. The junctions of the bamboo cane trusses do not use expensive metal pieces but are fixed by wooden dowels and elastic connections. The purlins and rafters are also made of bamboo cane with a diameter of about 50 mm and are fixed to the trusses with wooden dowels and connecting pieces. The fibre-cement pantiles are fixed to roofing battens made of split bamboo cane. These tiles can be produced by the locals themselves and are thus extremely economical in comparison with the normal corrugated Eternit sheets that contain asbestos. Deep roof overhangs protect the rendered brickwork walls and the bamboo-clad wall elements from the driving rain.

► The traditional process of smoking and flaming over gas burners protects the bamboo sections from rot. Prefabricated windows and doors made of yellow flamed bamboo cane using a 'rattan' construction method with woven corner connections are placed in the wall openings. These elements allow air to pass through and thus allow the natural ventilation of the interior.

► A dry toilet with an adjoining composting pit for wastewater provides for the disposal of excrement with reduced water usage.

► A rainwater cistern placed at a cool position between the strip foundations feeds (by means of hand pumps, in some cases also electrical pumps) the elevated supply tanks above the tap connections in the kitchen and bathroom.

Summary:

This starter house with a floor area of about 10 square metres (3.60 m x 3.60 m) covers half the area of the single-family house that in its final form will consist of two rooms as well as a kitchen and bathroom. The first building phase could be completed in the short period of only 15 days thanks to intensive cooperation between the residents of the favela and the architecture students from Rio-Niterói and Constance.

The building costs (material costs only) for a two-room house with a floor area of *c*. 20 square metres is around 2,000 real (approx. US $2,200). By comparison, a house of the same size in the favelas built of the usual, relatively expensive materials, such as concrete, sawn timber, metal fittings, industrially produced roofing battens and standard windows and doors, costs around 5,000 real (approx. US $5,500). The pilot project and the completed economic favela house have been positively evaluated by the future users as well as by 'specialists'. The house is now occupied and seems to be proving its worth. Two further houses based on the same principle are also under construction. This form of economically favourable construction apparently meets with the residents' approval and could indeed be repeated as a larger series, which was the original aim.

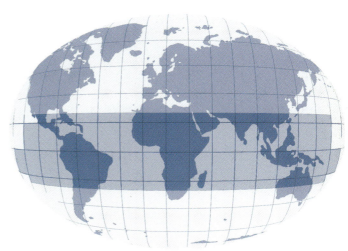

Urban Planning and Housing in East Asia and China

The old contrasts with the new in modern-day Shanghai

A model view of the megacity Shanghai (above) and the
360-meters-high Jin Mao Tower (below) with its 88 stories
has become a landmark of this district.

East Asia – Dense and High

Eckhart Ribbeck

Dynamic regions determine the culture of an epoch while at the same time creating new models in architecture and urban planning. In this sense Europe dominated the 19th century and North America the 20th. Today, an increasingly important region is the Far East, where new standards in urbanism and architecture are being set for the 21st century. Within a few decades East Asia has experienced a spectacular rise accompanied by urbanisation on a massive scale. In China alone, where the majority of the population still lives in the rural areas, there will be around 250 million new city dwellers in the next 20 years. The new metropolises are not growing slowly and continuously, like historic cities, but in rapid leaps – with ambitious projects acting as the pacemakers. The goal of these cities is to move into the league of global players, regardless of the cost, and to become centres for the international flow of money and trade and locations for future-oriented investment.

What are these new cities like? Following the example set by Hong Kong, they are dense and high and in many respects outside our familiar standards. Whereas Europe, respectful of its historic inheritance and warned by the rigid modernism of the 1960s and '70s, adopts the new urban and building typologies with caution, the boom cities in Asia believe in a spectacular future and progress.

As this new urbanism takes little account of historic heritage, the boom cities are often accused of reckless urban planning that destroys historic and cultural identity. However, this could be a misunderstanding: the young societies of East Asia are focussing on the future, because the past is associated with hunger, misery, colonial domination and communist stagnation. At the same time, their cultural identity still seems so strong that it does not need to rely

so heavily on the support of old cities. This is also evident in Japan, which, despite its strong cultural traditions, cultivates a very free approach to architecture and urban planning. It is not so much the historic old towns or careful urban renovation that are seen as important but super towers, artificial urban islands and other futuristic projects.

In contrast to the compact European city with its moderate density and height, or the North American city with its vertical central business district and endless flat suburbs, in the fast growing cities of East Asia almost everything is both high-rise and high-density. This applies in particular to the city centre, a kind of urban high-performance engine, but also the satellite towns and industrial areas mostly show an extreme density. Clearly, urban planning aims at a capital- and technology-intensive city which anticipates what all densely populated regions will have to deal with: increasing masses of people in a limited urban area. It seems that planners in East Asia are fully aware that the mighty flood of people streaming into the cities in the next decades cannot be dealt with using traditional urban models. These new cities are not being formed by a historically grown citizenry and through public participation but by technocratic decisions, public-private partnership and joint ventures, whereby the investors enjoy great freedom in the creation of new urban and building typologies. Large urban areas are taken over by private developers and filled with comprehensive development projects that promise maximum profit. As a result, many buildings seem like a hybrid between the European block and the North American tower intended to create high density and an intensive mix of uses.

Intensive commerce is located in the basements of such buildings, grouped around huge atriums and halls, while the towers are occupied by offices, hotels and luxury apartments. Often, groups of buildings blend together to form 'metropolitan complexes' that are closely linked to each other and to the public transport system. The separation of building from street vanishes, as does the distinction between private and public space, and with this the character of the traditional city also disappears. The labyrinthine containers may occasionally recall the 19th-century shopping arcades, a model that is now revived and enlarged several times. Public life moves into these protected environments, that is, into climatically, socially and economically conditioned buildings or to artificial plazas and urban gardens which are only apparently public; in fact, they are an integral part of the private developments.

As it is almost impossible to manage the enormous masses of pedestrians and motorised vehicles on a single level, the traffic is separated and layered. Elevated galleries, arcades, skywalks and garden-decks replace the conventional street and the classic pavement. For the pedestrian the abrupt changes from high to low and from inside to outside offer completely new experiences. Here, too, the model seems to be Hong Kong, where an elevated pedestrian system already extends through the entire city core and is closely connected to the underground railway, bus and ferry stations. Close residential districts are also connected: in the morning, kilometre-long escalators and travelators run towards the central business district and in the evening, in the other direction back to the apartment towers.

What makes Hong Kong, Shanghai and other East Asian boom cities fascinating despite their futuristic scenery are the extreme urban contrasts: the ultra modern city, remnants of the colonial town, overcrowded China Town, desolate residential areas from the socialist era, 30-storey satellite towns... Nowhere in the world do large cities offer such great diversity which, however, now threatens to disappear in the course of the building boom.

Urban development in East Asia cannot be measured by conventional rules: instead of history, the future is celebrated, instead of harmony, the stark contrast, instead of bourgeois restraint, aggressive competitiveness and vitality. This all reflects an optimistic view of the future and the keenness of national and international investors to participate in this boom. It may even seem that the futuristic urban visions that were created in Europe in the 1960s, but which were later forgotten, are now being realised in East Asia. In this sense this region is a laboratory for a new metropolitan architecture and a post-European urbanism that responds to the urban challenge in a new way.

What perspectives does this urbanism have and how can it be evaluated from the viewpoints of its climatic suitability and long-term sustainability? As the traditional cities show, high density is nothing new in Chinese towns. What is new is the extreme verticality that reduces drastically the possibilities of climatically appropriate building in the traditional sense. The focus is no longer on an intensive dialogue between inside and outside, between the built and natural environment, but on complex interior worlds with an artificially controlled climate.

In regions that are exposed to wet heat and tropical storms for many months of the year this makes sense. Hong Kong is certainly no conventional city, but a kind of human 'termites' nest' that resists the tropical climate by means of an extensive system of protected environments. In similar fashion, large areas of the city have already blended to form a gigantic climatic shell under which life is being lived intensively. Of course this 'urban machine' is not planned for eternity but to be changed and adapted in a rapid rhythm – an artificial organism that constantly renews itself, internally and externally.

In an increasingly urbanised world dense and high cities have the advantage of being able to keep the urban sprawl within reasonable limits, which in a country like China would devour immense space if a scattered urban pattern were applied. The challenge

A typical multi-storey apartment building facing south with the ground floor often used for commercial purposes. The individual apartments range from 70 – 150 m², have an international modern design, and have little in common with a traditional Chinese ground plan.

to accommodate a few hundred million new urban dwellers does not allow low-rise, low-density suburbs, although these might appear more human than 20- to 30-storey apartment blocks. So far, no one can say whether this urbanism is more or less sustainable than the conventional city, where some important questions are also still open. North American suburbs are extremely questionable considering their excessive consumption of energy, the wasteful use of land and to over-motorisation. The 'compact' European city also suffers urban sprawl and fragmentation, apart from the fact that it is tied to a long history and cultural circumstances that cannot simply be transplanted in other regions of the world.

Of course, the urban model which is applied in booming East Asia also brings with it a great risk, because to produce forcefully an entirely new urbanism need not necessarily prove successful. If the boom slows down, then nothing will remain of the East Asian high-tech city but a torso in which the same phenomena that characterise other megacities may also appear: increasing urban poverty and a periphery that is increasingly split up into prosperous gated communities and poor, uncontrolled settlements.

Beijing – Fine Living

When masses of people stream into the gigantic halls of the military museum in Beijing these days, then the attraction is generally not so much the weapons of the Chinese Revolution but the housing fair held there at regular intervals. Several hundred projects are presented, generally large housing estates that are built and marketed by investors from China, Hong Kong and Taiwan. Those interested are usually young couples who collect stacks of brochures and pamphlets and admire the oversized posters and models. In Beijing, a true 'apartment hunger' seems to have broken out that is setting urban society in a social and spatial motion previously undreamed of.

The relatively free housing market has existed only for the last 15 years. Once a uniform socialist mass, urban society is now sorting itself anew. In this process the fair plays an important role: it provides an overview of the enormous number of projects and at the same time offers new models for consumption and status-oriented living – a new lifestyle for the aspiring middle class. The urban population in Beijing that can afford a new dwelling is estimated at around 25 per cent. This means that over a million families are looking for a new home. This explains the boom in housing construction, which is encouraged by favourable loans because the state is also interested in a flourishing economy.

The projects presented generally lie in the core city of Beijing, mostly on the 3rd, 4th or 5th ring where there is practically no restriction on building height. Particularly attractive are the north of Beijing with the Olympia Park, the university district in the north-west, as well as the east, where a new central business district is currently being built. But investors are increasingly discovering the less attractive south and south-east of the city, as land prices are lower there and the planned urbanisation corridor to Taijin suggests that there will be extensive public investment in this district. Better and worse residential districts are already developing in Beijing – a clear indication of the social and spatial segregation that will alter the city considerably in the medium term. Important factors when buying a new home are: the price of the apartment, the image of a particular zone, and a good public transport system, whereby both the existing and the planned metro lines play a key role.

Investors usually plan and build large housing areas with several hundred apartments. The projects are placed in the existing urban structure with little regard for its inhabitants, because the calculation is obviously that the old surroundings – mostly desolate old housing or industrial areas – will in any case vanish. The massive construction of housing naturally attracts commercial activities so that new commercial streets and shopping centres grow up almost spontaneously in the neighbourhood of large projects and secure the market of the better-off population.

In the eastern core city, large project clusters have already formed. However, these new housing areas do not blend together but separate themselves rigorously from each other by means of walls and gateways. This is not a new phenomenon in Beijing: the historic quarters were also protected by walls and gates, as were the socialist working and living units. It is, therefore, not surprising that Chinese investors and urban planners also tend to see the city more as an addition of semi-autonomous settlement cells and less as a continuous system of streets and spaces, such as, for example, the traditional European city. Separate and enclosed housing projects not only continue a long tradition but also offer the investor many advantages. A central axis and a symmetrical layout also offer a robust concept that allows a large number of buildings to be ordered in a simple and rapid way.

Whether the new gated communities represent an urban inheritance or a new phenomenon that is beginning to fragment the Chinese city is rarely discussed in depth in the public discourse. To people only lately released from socialist uniformity it seems completely natural that everyone who can afford to now looks for a new apartment. Not only income groups but generations also are moving apart, because it is mostly young families that move into the new buildings, while their parents and grandparents remain in the familiar old districts. Urban policy hardly intervenes in the segregation process, although the inhabitants of demolished old buildings are offered help in finding a new home. So far it remains unclear whether the new housing units will turn out to be permeable, that is, whether outsiders will be able to enter or cross it freely. Walls and guarded gateways have created facts, but naturally the municipal authorities still have the power to open up the gated communities through clear urban regulations, so that the city does not become just a collection of isolated housing cells. Education and health are still controlled by the state in communist China, although one occasionally finds private nursery schools. Naturally, the privileged sectors of society will attempt to separate themselves from the public system as soon as their income level allows them to do so. If the state yields to such pressure then another foundation of China's socialist society will crumble and there will be no further impediment to the formation of exclusive luxury ghettos equipped with private schools and leisure facilities.

As there exists little overall planning, investors fulfil an important function in replacing the old and decaying districts and creating new housing areas and housing typologies according to which society is rearranging itself. Naturally, this activity is profit-oriented and often produces a kind of decorative architecture, which promises an elevated status and lifestyle. At the same time, these 'artificial districts' also allow for a sense of identification and provide a new spatial order, which is obviously accepted and appreciated by the upwardly mobile sectors of the population.

From the planning stage to the actual sale of an apartment building rarely takes more than a year. The first apartment buildings generally serve as advertising, so that subsequent apartments can often be sold before the actual construction begins. In certain cases the developer must produce at least the constructive framework before he can start to sell apartments. Wherever possible, commercial uses are integrated in the project in order to max-imise profits. In central locations these often take the form of large department stores and office towers, and the ground floor of the apartment buildings is often reserved for shops.

In the 13-million megacity, gardens and parks are a luxury and green, open spaces therefore play an important role in the building projects because they help to sell the apartments. This is also indicated by the flowery names of the projects of which the word 'garden' is an essential part, for example, 'Heavenly Gardens' or 'Pearl Paradise Garden'. *Feng shui* sculptures, which are supposed to bring luck, are also placed in the outdoor spaces. However, it

remains to be seen whether the successful residents of the newly-built districts will use their outdoor areas as intensively as the courtyards and streets of the old city, or whether they will instead prefer to spend their leisure time in the new shopping centres, theme parks or at McDonald's.

A car is an important part of the upward move in society, which is why investor-built housing increas-ingly provides parking spaces and underground garages. This is something relatively new in Beijing; even only a few years ago no one would have predicted that private motorisation would happen so quickly. Quite clearly, the increase in the number of cars also alters the layout of the projects, as increasing amounts of space must be reserved for roads and parking spaces.

The new housing typology extends from the 30-storey tower to multi-storey blocks and villas in a 'Victorian style', whereby detached family houses are to be found only in the periphery of Beijing. How-ever different the buildings may be, most projects have in common the basic urban concept: an intro-verted housing area, a north-south axis, and as many south-facing dwellings as possible. Facing south is almost obligatory, as any other orientation means that the dwelling will fetch a lower price. This ancient building tradition, which is to be found in Eastern and Central Asia as far as Iran, follows a simple logic. When low in the sky, the sun is a natu-ral source of heating during the cold winters; in the hot summers, when the sun stands high, the building can be protected by simple means, for example, by a projecting roof. This and other traditions were refined in China over the course of centuries into the *feng shui* theory, which at times acquires an almost religious character.

Speculative housing is naturally oriented primarily towards the market, but nevertheless has continued the principle of south-facing dwellings. This explains why the closed 'European block' is hardly to be found, although here and there attempts are made to introduce this model into Chinese urban planning. To this extent, 'gated communities' and south-facing dwellings seem to be the only traditions evident in new housing. Of course, the principle of energy recovery in winter and simple shade in summer could also be used in multi-storey buildings, but because the façades are more often designed according to decorative rather than environmental considerations, possible climatic advantages are generally not exploited. Naturally, with the spread of Western lifestyle, housing priorities can change. The morning sun on the breakfast table, the evening sun after a long working day – that is to say, east-west oriented apartments could also become attractive in future. These, however, require an architecture that is climatically well planned, otherwise artificial air-conditioning would become essential.

A 100-square-metre apartment in a good location costs around 60,000 euros. This seems reasonable but for buyers who on average rarely earn monthly salaries of 600 euros it is far from cheap. Naturally, comfort, security and the expensive design of outdoor space also have their price, which raises apartment costs considerably. Therefore, most people have to take out long-term loans, which means that they depend on steady and well-paid jobs in the future. Apartment sizes vary between 80 and 150 square metres, whereby a 100-square-metre apartment is regarded as rather modest. This is a clear indication of the social gulf in the metropolis, in which millions of families still live in single rooms. The new apartments are modern and functional; apparently without characteristics that are specifically Chinese, although occasionally a statue of Buddha decorates the living room. This does not necessarily indicate any lack of cultural identity but rather reflects the buyers wish, after years of uniform and desolate living conditions, to live according to a modern and international standard. The apart-

ments are equipped with a central heating system, but the owners must install the air-conditioning needed in the hot summers. Energy is still relatively cheap in China and therefore its economic use does not yet play an important role in planning and building. Poor insulation of walls and windows, as well as defective construction, represent serious problems. Better design, increased experience and, above all, rising energy prices will certainly change this situation, as poorly constructed and insulated buildings will become too expensive in the long term.

Despite the aggressive advertising at the housing fairs, excesses of architectural style and design are kept within certain limits. The postmodern kitsch that one often sees in many other cities is hardly to be found any more in Beijing, as considerable experience has been reached in the handling of housing projects. One project generation is following another, and in only a few years there have been noticeable leaps in quality. This makes any criticism one might make of current building relative. On the other hand, many projects are ageing rapidly and will soon fall out of fashion.

The commercial housing projects and gated communities, of which hundreds are currently being created in Beijing, are very much comparable to those in capitalist countries, but on the other hand spontaneous settlements of the poor, such as those found in other southern cities, do not yet exist on the periphery of Beijing. But this could also change in the future if the state hands over the housing market completely to commercial interests. The housing shortage of the poor would then increase and lead to the polarisation between luxury quarters and poverty ghettos that is typical of most southern countries.

Nanjing road, Shanghai.

Urban expansion in Pudong, Shanghai
and its commercial centre (middle)
Urban expansion in Hangzhou (below).

190

Planning and building in the Chinese metropolises
Peter Cheret

As a result of the policy of opening up the country, formulated around 1978, and, at the latest, since the introduction of the 'socialist market economy', from 1992 onwards, large regions of China have begun to develop at almost breakneck speed. It is not only existing large cities such as Shanghai or Beijing but also smaller cities in the provinces that are suddenly being transformed into industrial metropolises. The economic boom is accompanied by a redistribution of the population throughout the country. Increasing numbers of people from remote regions are looking for and finding employment in the boom areas. The general standard of living is also rising as a result of the continuous increase in productive power. The demand for goods and services is growing and, in accordance with classic market-economy principles, is leading to a steady expansion of the supply.

One of the central problems in China's newly developing cities is how to build large amounts of reasonably priced housing. Since the founding of the People's Republic there have been a number of different approaches to the rationalisation and standardisation of housing construction. Initially, at the time of the first five-year plan (1953-57), construction methods as well as housing models from the Soviet Union were adopted. In all cities, large new residential districts consisting of multi-storey housing were created. After the split with the Soviet Union in 1960, the existing standard floor plans were adapted to meet specifically Chinese requirements. With the aim of preserving the maximum amount of fertile ground, from 1966 until Mao's death in 1976, prefabricated system high-rise housing blocks with only a few different types of minimal floor plans were erected on the periphery of the

large cities. This approach was altered during the reform era and in the changing political climate that prevailed from 1978 onwards: the floor plans became more flexible and the building methods were adapted to provide higher levels of domestic comfort.

With the introduction and application of free-market principles to the purchase of dwellings and the establishment of a system of subsidised housing for middle and lower income groups, today there is available an entire series of individualised floor plans in many different types of buildings. In contrast to the dominant ideology during the founding era of the People's Republic the current trend in terms of structure and construction is away from large-scale industrial mass production. The construction system using prefabricated walls and floors proved too inflexible and is no longer used. As a rule, the shells – generally skeleton frame structures of concrete and masonry – are nowadays erected using conventional building methods and the details are, by and large, standardised. The basis of all planning in China, from the overall structure to general building construction and down to services, is provided by standard detail manuals that are issued and kept up to date by institutes established especially for this purpose. These institutes are organised on a decentralised basis and are in constant contact with large, state planning offices, where building construction methods suited to the market are newly developed or improved. Reflecting the structure of these institutes, there are some manuals that are used throughout China, whereas others are used only in specific provinces and a number are valid only for certain cities. In general, this collection of manuals determines standards at the provincial level. For example, the 'Building Construction Series 88J', issued by the 'Northern Region Office for Building Design Standardisation', is used in eight northern and western provinces that all belong to the same climatic zone.

The major advantage offered by this standard work lies in its overall validity and application. The planners do not develop the details themselves, they simply take them from the manual and apply them to the detail planning. The planning period required, even for large projects, is thus reduced to a few weeks. Construction companies have tested these standard solutions for all building details on numerous occasions and their costs can therefore be easily calculated. Without this extensive standardisation and simplification of the planning and construction process, which allows costs to be simply estimated and controlled, it would not be possible to cope with the enormous volume of building in China's boom regions. However, it should be said that in comparison with the developed industrialised countries the standard of building technology remains low. The levels of sound and thermal insulation laid down in the Chinese standards and building regulations are not only far below those found in Europe, but the built structures often do not meet even the local minimum requirements. The building shells are generally unsuited for coping with the effects of periodic climatic variations. The basic demands of building science are often ignored, and thermal bridges and windows that are not properly weathertight are accepted. As a result of the general lack of protection against summertime heat, individual air-conditioning appliances are standard items. The high level of energy consumption in the major population centres is leading to more and more cuts and shortages in the power supply during the summer.

Unfortunately, the general quality of building suffers from the overheated nature of construction activity. It is not unusual to see new buildings with clearly visible defects in their primary structure. The same applies to the interior, where the transition between the surfaces of different materials is often handled in a visually clumsy and functionally inadequate way and where the service runs seem unconsidered and improvised. All these defects can make the building age extremely quickly. In addition to these aesthetic problems, such buildings almost inevitably require regular and costly maintenance, which means tying up future capital.

Traditional Chinese settlement on water (opposite page)

Lilong area in Shanghai (right)

The opportunity to experiment with different directions in the wake of the dynamic development in the construction of new cities is, alas, not being exploited. Urban planning in general is following principles that in Europe were laid to rest in the 1960s. There is an inherent, clearly visible contradiction in trying to build the city of the future with the constructional means of the 19th century. Equally scurrilous are many of the major projects that resemble stage sets and imitate international high-tech architecture, while others are adorned with stylistic elements borrowed from the history of European architecture from antiquity to modernism. It is equally significant and surprising that in a country with a history dating back many thousands of years no individual native impulses are set and that, given the enormous overall volume of building, not even a few Chinese personalities have been able to establish themselves with an internationally recognised oeuvre. Even though traditional architecture and anonymous building lie well beyond the present-day field of vision, they still preserve and offer principles relating to climatically appropriate building and the local cultural identity that could be transformed and applied to modern building.

The dilemma is clear: regulated standardisation is, on the one hand, the guarantee for unrestricted growth of the volume of construction. On the other hand, all planning activities that aim to raise construction and design standards involve a departure from the generally accepted technology and therefore demand specialist, one-off constructions. The effort involved in planning and the length of the planning period increase dramatically as the detailing becomes more complex. The same applies to the length of the construction phase and, naturally, also to costs. However, it is foreseeable that the issue of an improvement in the quality of building, above all with regard to climatically appropriate building, will have to be tackled. With the rise in the standard of living, the demand for greater quality grows and the supply available on the market expands.

The goal of China's metropolises is already clear: a step up into the league of the global cities and towards attractiveness for seminal international investments. In the long term, this aim cannot be achieved without an intact environment, town planning and architecture on an international level and an individual cultural identity.

Changzhou Village in Hangzhou, People's Republic of China

International architecture competition for a housing development for 8,000 elderly people
Design: Cheret and Bozic Architects, Stuttgart

Hangzhou, the capital of Zhejiang Province, can look back over a long history. With the construction of the Emperor's Canal in the early 7th century the city developed into an important centre for the exchange and transfer of goods and subsequently developed into one of the most prosperous commercial cities. Marco Polo describes Hangzhou – which he calls Quinzhai – as the most beautiful and elegant city in the world with its magnificent streets, buildings and canals. Today, Hangzhou, which lies about 200 kilometres to the south-east of Shanghai and has a population of 1.4 million, is an upwardly striving industrial city developing through almost unrestricted growth. As in the time of Marco Polo the production of silk still plays an important role.
Hangzhou lies on the legendary West Lake, whose praises are sung in literature and which represents an ideal Chinese landscape. In more recent times, large areas of the shoreline were developed with further pavilions, pagodas, artificial dams and small islands.

The competition

The architecture competition was created as part of plans by the Hangzhou authorities to build a housing development in the north of the city for about 8,000 elderly people. Three foreign and three Chinese architects' practices were invited to submit suitable designs. In addition to one American and one English practice the office of Peter Cheret and Jelena Bozic from Stuttgart also submitted an entry.
The initiators of the competition were the city of Hangzhou, together with FOUND Real Estate, an investor that operates throughout China.
The site made available was about 50 hectares in area. The terrain is hilly, largely undeveloped and for the most part covered with bamboo forest.
The background to the project was to create living space for elderly people who are not in need of nursing care, that is to say, by and large, people from the generation of 'single-child parents' whose first members are now reaching retirement age.

Design concept

A description of the concept behind the project submitted by the Stuttgart architects is presented below. The architectural aims evolved out of the local, climatic and cultural conditions to create a complex overall urban figure.

Urban planning concept

The site, with its rich growth of bamboo forest, is a fascinating, almost untouched natural area. It was intended that the new buildings should preserve this quality as far as possible. Another primary idea was to articulate the mass of apartments into social units of reasonable size.

The product of these two primary considerations was the idea to create in the bamboo forest a number of clearings of equal size to be developed with 'villages' for between 500 and 600 inhabitants. The position of the clearings was determined according to the nature of the local topography.

System of streets and routes

The concept also called for the creation of a street and pedestrian network. Whereas the road, like the villages, was generated from the existing topographical situation, the footpaths were laid out in a way that exploits the quality of the landscape.

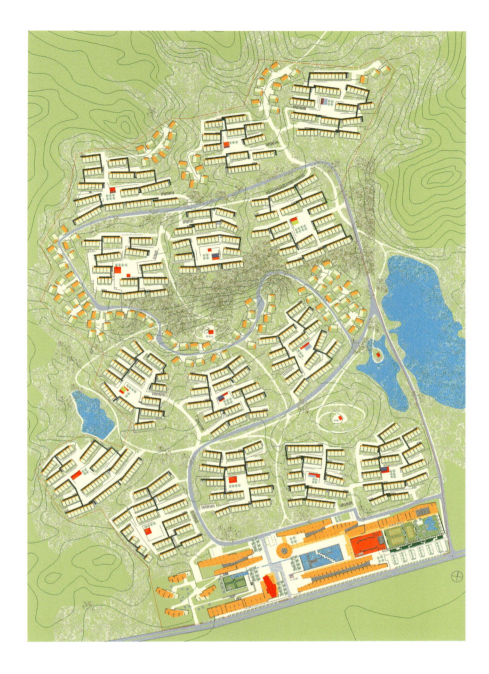

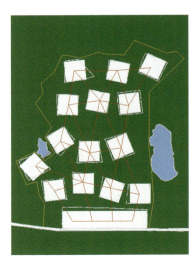
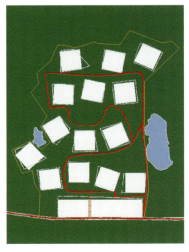
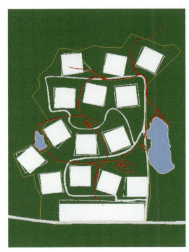

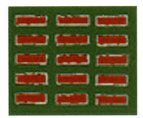 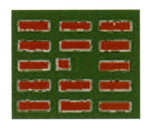 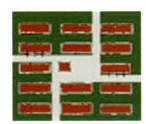 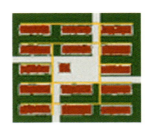 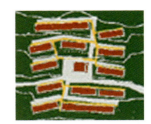

Old village structure

The historic Chinese town developed on the basis of a clearly recognisable geometric and architectural order. The regulations governing the building of houses were laid down in the Han era (206 BC to 220 AD) and remain valid to the present day. The basic scheme of north-south oriented rows was adopted and transformed. In a first intervention the centre was defined as a public space by modifying one of the rows. The next intervention was the system of the public routes. The position of the individual rows of houses in relation to each other and, consequently, the entire spatial configuration was a product of the existing topography. In this way it was possible to develop village structures that vary within a regular system, analogous to the historic city.

The construction of the buildings

The traditional method of construction in Chinese architecture is the timber-frame building. Based on this system, courtyard complexes were developed that were enclosed by walls. Borrowing from these traditional structures, and with the aim of keeping the technical complexity of the building construction

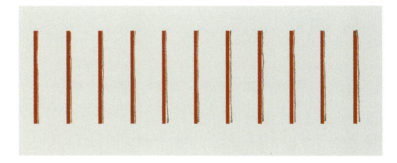

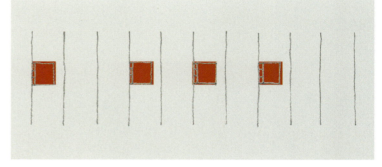

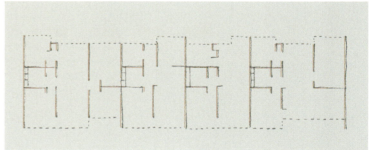

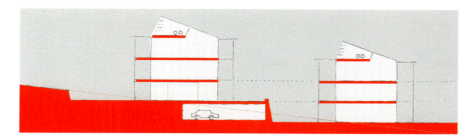

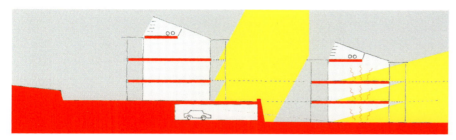

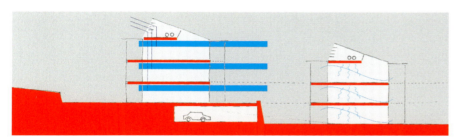

as simple as possible, the housing design uses a system of cross walls. The sanitary cells, whose size and fittings are uniform, can be positioned differently in the various dwelling types.

Building typology

The buildings are generally three storeys high. Analogous to the traditional Chinese city all dwelling units are accessed directly from outside – generally from a deck on the north side. On the south side there is a frame-like structure on which climbing plants can grow and which offers protection from the sun and supports the balconies. The building material used is bamboo that was cut when making the clearings and that allows playfully light structures to be made. In addition, two layers of bamboo canes were mounted on the exterior walls, where they improve the insulation and in summer provide increased protection against overheating.

Building-energy concept

Zhejiang Province lies in a moderate, warm and humid climatic zone with winter temperatures of slightly over freezing point, average summer temperatures of up to 30°C, and with high air-humidity levels. As a rule, buildings are not provided with heating systems. In summer, individual air-conditioning appliances are generally used. In Hangzhou, this leads at present to excessive demands on the electricity network and to regular power cuts. In a further analogy to traditional building an energy concept was developed that adopts the basic principles of intelligent vernacular architecture:

- ► Exploitation of the sloping site and the natural movement of air
- ► Open building structures to the north and south that can be well ventilated
- ► Correct dimensioning of the solar protection. While the hot summer sun cannot penetrate the interior of the building, the low winter sun can enter deep inside.
- ► Adjustable shafts in the interior of the buildings have a chimney effect that improves the natural ventilation.

Building circulation

The individual rows of buildings are placed on terraces made in the landscape in such a way that the individual levels can be connected by footbridges. A small number of lifts are suitable for the disabled and can ensure barrier-free access to all dwellings.

Towards a new architecture for the Tropics

In the year 2005, six thousand million human beings inhabited the earth of which five thousand million live in the Tropics and only one thousand million live in the temperate regions of the world. According to UNESCO population projection an estimated eight thousand million people will live in the Tropics in 2020, three thousand million in India and Africa alone. By contrast, the number of people living in the temperate regions will remain constant at around one thousand million, most in Europe and North America.

The increasing spread of urbanisation – a result of industrial development, population explosion and the flight from the country of large sectors of the population in search of a better life – has wide-ranging consequences for the expansion of the megacities with dense urban spaces for production, workplaces, administration buildings, health and community services.

Less than ten per cent of the world's population lived in urban areas at the beginning of the 20th century. According to UNESCO, there will be more than five thousand million people living in cities by 2025, two-thirds of them in developing nations. By the year 2020, there will be 33 megacities around the world, 27 of them in the developing world, and 19 in Asia alone.

Because of rapid population growth and urbaniza-tion, meeting the basic needs of the world's people, especially those in Third World nations, will pose serious challenges for governments, industry, agricultural producers and the global construction industry. Enormous construction efforts on a scale never seen before – as are currently in progress in China – will be needed to meet these needs.

However, new concepts and ideas should be devel-oped in order to avoid the excessive application of European and American building standards and practices in tropical environments for which they are often not suited. These new concepts must take into account the local economic, social and climatic conditions of an environment. This principle should apply to official public building programmes as well as to anonymous architecture.

This increase in urban density today means that in many parts of the world ecological issues are being ignored or abandoned. The intensive use of building sites, the stacking of living and work spaces and the increasing density of traffic leads to urban and build-ing structures that are based on American models from the 1940s and '50s, which require an intensive use of technology and disregard the level of energy consumption and its effect on the environment. The invention of air-conditioning has ensured that large buildings and high-rises can be supplied with fresh air as well as with sufficient cooling and heating energy. From an environmental viewpoint, the use of around 300–400 KWh/m^2 per year to provide this technically-produced comfort is simply too high. Furthermore, in the hot climatic zone of the Tropics the expensive use of air-conditioning for an architec-ture based on models from the First World is no longer economically viable. The amount of energy that such systems require is simply not available in these countries.

On the other hand, the energy actually available is, as a rule, more urgently required for tasks such as the economic development of the country in terms of industry and manufacturing rather than for the air-conditioning of badly planned apartment and office blocks.

In the future it will no longer be viable to operate buildings with inappropriate climatic concepts. For a dwelling house in an African country with a floor area of around 140 square metres, three 2,000-watt air-conditioning appliances produce monthly elec-tricity bills of about US $120. This clearly makes little economic sense. This same principle is true for public buildings in many developing countries, many of which are constructed as prestige objects with funds from development aid and eventually fall into disuse for economic reasons.

The tropical cities and buildings of the future must adopt an ecological, economic architecture that uses increasingly expensive resources more sparingly and employ new concepts to make living in these environments more humane. Technical aids should be employed in an ecological and economic manner and the possibilities of sustainability offered by natural, climatically responsive building should be developed further. Throughout the world, we currently use primary energy that took millions of years to produce in the form of fossil fuel. Sixty per cent of this energy is used in the building sector, over half of it for cooling, heating and lighting, with serious consequences for the level of CO_2 emissions in our atmosphere and, accordingly, a negative effect on the global climate. This situation lends a new dimension to the task of building in the Tropics.

The ecological and economic viewpoints of climatically appropriate and sustainable building should, however, be evaluated not only regionally (for the tropical Third World) but also globally in terms of concern and responsibility for the environment. The international agreement set forth in the Kyoto Protocol is an important step in the direction of global environmental responsibility. Unfortunately it has not received support worldwide.

In the future, the living standard and economic development of our society will become increasingly dependent on the health of the environment, on the global climate, the level of population growth, and global energy reserves. Scientists have predicted a rise in global temperatures and its negative effects. According to these predictions, the world will have to contend with the effects of more and more weather-related disasters, melting glaciers, and the consequences of rising sea levels, especially in the monsoon-affected coastal regions of Asia.

Of greater significance, however, is the aspect of a humane architecture, which represents the original purpose of architecture: "To create shelter and protection and thus distinguish man's surroundings from the natural environment", as the well-known author of *Architecture without Architects*, Bernhard Rudofsky, stated – in other words, to protect the privacy and intimacy of the individual in the community of the family and the city. Equally, forms of living together according to old and new traditions, rites and religious observances should be taken into account in creating the mesh of urban space.

This book is also aimed at the emerging architects of the Tropics, that they may be inspired by the traditional architecture of their ancestors to develop a new regional creativity, to break free of the stranglehold of schematic international solutions and to advance towards a new architecture of the Tropics, a 'new tropicalism' as part of the culture of a country.

Architecture of the Rainforest

Heinrich Barth, *Reisen und Entdeckungen in Nord- und Zentral-afrika in den Jahren 1849–1855*.

Bier, *Asien – Strasse – Haus*, Stuttgart 1992.

Dupperey, *Voyage of the Coquille*, 1821.

Leo Frobenius, *The Voice of Africa*, Berlin 1912.

Wolfgang Lauber, 'Wohnbauten in den Favelas von Rio de Janeiro', in *Trialog* 4 / 1996.

—— (ed.), *Palaces and Compounds in the Grasslands of Cameroon*, Stuttgart 1990.

——, *Deutsche Architektur in Kamerun*, Stuttgart 1988.

——, *Deutsche Architektur in Togo*, Stuttgart 1993.

Georg Lippsmeier, *Tropenbau*, Munich 1980.

Sybil Moholy-Nagy, *Native Genius in Anonymous Architecture*, 1962.

Guy Philippart de Foy, Christian Seignobos, *Les Pygmees d'Afrique Centrale*, 1984.

Bernhard Rudofsky, *Architecture without Architects*, New York, 1964.

Claude Tardits, *Le Palais Royal de Foumban*

Architecture of the Savannah

Gérard Beaudoin, *Les Dogons du Mali*, Paris 1984.

Rogier M. A. Bedaux, *Djenné*, Leiden 1994.

Rogier M. A. Bedaux, 'Tellem, Reconnaissance archéologique d'une culture de l'Ouest africain au Moyen Âge'

'Recherches architectoniques', *Journal de la Société des Africanistes*, XLII,2, 1972, pp. 103–185.

Rogier M. A. Bedaux, A. G. Lange, 'Tellem, Reconnaissance archéologique d'une culture de l'Ouest africain au Moyen Âge, La poterie', *Journal de la Société des Africanistes*, LIII, 1983, pp. 5–59.

Jean Paul Bourdier, Trinh T. Minh-ha, *African Spaces*, New York, London 1985.

Gert Chesi, *Architektur und Mythos Lehmbauten in Schwarzafrika*, Innsbruck 1995.

Louis Desplagnes, *Le Plateau central nigérien, une mission archéologique et ethnographique au Soudan français*, Paris 1907.

Jean Dethie, *Lehmarchitektur*, exhibition catalogue, Centre Pompidou Paris / Architecture Museum Frankfurt/M., Munich 1982.

Walter Ferstl, 'Unbekannte Meisterwerke der Baukunst Z-aktuell', *Bundesverband der Deutschen Ziegelindustrie*, Bonn 1984.

Annemarie Fiedermutz-Laun, Dorothee Gruner, Eike Haberland, Karl-Heinz Striedter, *Aus Erde geformt*, ed. by Frobenius Institut Frankfurt/M., Mainz 1990.

René Gardi, *Auch im Lehmhaus lässt sich's leben*, Graz 1973.

Marcel Griaule, *Dieu d'eau, entretiens avec Ogotemmêli*, Paris 1948, reprint 1966.

Prussin Labelle, *The architecture of Islam in West Africa*, African Arts, 1968.

——, *Sudanese architecture and the Manding*, African Arts 1970.

Wolfgang Lauber (ed.), *Architektur der Dogon*, Munich 1998.

Héléne Leloup / William Rubin / Richard Serra / Georg Baselitz, Statuaire Dogon, Strasbourg 1994

Pierre Maas, Gert Mommer, *Djenné*, Eindhoven, 1992.

Charles Monteil, *Monographie de Djenné*, Tulle 1903, reprint 1932.

Paul Oliver, *Shelter in Africa*, London 1976.

Jürgen Schneider, *Am Anfang die Erde*, Frankfurt/M., Cologne 1985.

Tito and Sandro Spini, *Togu Na*, New York 1977.

Convention concernant la protection du patrimoine mondial, culturel et naturel, Paris, 16 November 1972, WHC Paris, UNESCO.

Gerda Wangerin, *Bauaufnahme*, Wiesbaden 1992.

Nadine Wanjono, *Les Dogon*, Paris 1997.

Hans Wichmann, Jürgen Adam (eds.), *Architektur der Vergänglichkeit, Lehmbauten der Dritten Welt*, Neue Sammlung, Staatliches Museum für angewandte Kunst, Munich 1981.

On Modern Architecture

Boesiger-Girsberger, *Le Corbusier 1910–1965*, 1993.

Klaus Peter Gast, *Le Corbusier*, Basel/Berlin 2000.

Henrique E. Mindlin, *Neues Bauen in Brasilien*, Munich/New York 1956.

Glenn Murcutt, *Bauten und Projekte*; London/Berlin 1995.

Karl Petzold, *Bauen in den warmen Klimatem, Bauklimatische Grundlagen*, Leipzig 1985.

Rem Koolhaas, *Mutations Harvard Project on the City*, 2002.

Philipp Menser, *Sehnsucht nach Europa*, 2003.

Oscar Niemeyer, *The Curves of Time*, London 2000.

Renzo Piano, *Arquitectures sostenibles*, Barcelona 1998.

Eckart Ribbeck, Sergio Padilla, *Informal Modernism. Spontaneous Building in Mexico City*, 2002.

David Underwood, *Oscar Niemeyer and the Architecture of Brazil*, New York 1994.

Frank Lloyd Wright, *Bauten in Arizona*, Cologne 1991.

Torsten Warner, *Deutsche Architektur in China*, Berlin 1994.

Acknowledgements

We wish to thank the following academic institutions
for their support both of the research projects and
this publication:
Deutsche Forschungsgemeinschaft, Bonn
(German Research Foundation)
Deutscher Akademischer Austauschdienst, Bonn
(German Academic Exchange Service)
Kulturabteilung des Auswärtigen Amtes, Berlin
(Cultural Department of the German Foreign
Ministry)
UNESCO World Heritage Center, Paris
Association of Friends of the University of Applied
Sciences Constance
Institute for Applied Research of the University of
Applied Sciences Constance

We thank all of our students and colleagues
for their contributions to our research work,
especially Manfred von Mende, Stephan Romero,
Horst Teppert and Fritz Wilhelm.

The Faculty of Architecture and Urbanism,
University of Stuttgart

We received generous support from the following:
Scancem International ANS, Oslo, Norway
MAPS Geo Systems, Munich, Germany
Sto AG, Stuehlingen, Germany

We thank the people and the anonymous builders of
the countries involved for their friendly cooperation
during our field research trips and for handing on to
us the traditional knowledge of their regional, climatically appropriate architecture.

I wish also to thank my wife, Ute Sabine, and my
daughter, Alexandra Yatimba, for their help and
patient support during my work on this book.

The Contributors

Peter Cheret teaches in the Faculty of Architecture
and Urban Planning at the University of Stuttgart,
Germany. He is a practicing architect and a specialist in the field of wood construction.

Klaus K. J. Ferstl is a practicing architect in Dresden,
Germany, and taught at the Dresden University of
Technology. Extensive fieldwork and teaching in
Central Asia and Africa. He also works as a consult-
ant on Climate-Oriented Design and Energy-Efficient
Building.

Wolfgang Lauber is a practicing architect and
consultant. He has published widely in the field of
African architecture and currently teaches at the
University of Applied Sciences in Constance, and
the University of Stuttgart, Germany.

Eckhart Ribbeck teaches at the Faculty of Archi-
tecture and Urban Planning at the University of
Stuttgart, Germany. He heads the Department
SIAAL – Urban Planning in Asia, Africa and Latin
America – and has done extensive urban research
in Mexico and Brazil.

The photographs, plans and drawings contained in this publication are by Wolfgang Lauber, University of Constance, with the exception of those on the following pages:

11 (bottom), 36 (top), 56 (centre and bottom) Seraina Camenisch/ Antonia Schweitzer, Utwil; 32 (top), 36 (bottom right), 37 (centre), 128–29, 133 (left), 139 (bottom), 158–59, 164–65, 166, 168, 169, 171, 185 Eckhart Ribbeck, Stuttgart; 33 (bottom) Stephan Romero, Constance; 37 (top), 37 (bottom), 80-81, 180-182, 191, 192, 193, 194, 197 Peter Cheret, Stuttgart; 58-59 Michael Bier, Valparaiso; 63 (centre), 63 (bottom) Maps Geo Systems, Munich, 72 (top), 72 (centre), 72 (bottom) Oliver Oexle, Constance; 72 (plans, isometric) Klaus Schneider, Cologne; 116 (bottom), 118 (top left) Simon Velez, Bogota; 126 Händle; 127 Sto AG; 134 Torsten Warner, Vienna; 136 Antonia Schweitzer, Utwil; 137 Horst Teppert, Munich; 139 (drawings) Oscar Niemeyer, Rio de Janeiro; 138, 142, 144–45 Foundation Le Corbusier/VG Bildkunst, Bonn; 146–47 Reiner Blunck, Tübingen; 148–49 OMA, Rotterdam; 150 John Gollings, Melbourne; 150-151 Renzo Piano Building Workshop, Paris/Genoa; 153 (bottom) Dalla Corte Architects, Gottlieben; 154 Alexandra Mebus, Constance; 160 Stephanie Maze Woodfin Camp AG Focus, Hamburg

Endpapers (front): The village Ireli in Dogon country, Mali
Endpapers (back): The tropical rainforest in Cameroon
Page 2: A farmer's house in Zanzibar, Tanzania
Page 4: The palace forecourt in Ngaundere, northern Cameroon

Prestel Verlag
Königinstrasse 9, 80539 Munich
Tel. +49 (89) 38 17 09-0
Fax +49 (89) 38 17 09-35
www.prestel.de

Prestel Publishing Ltd.
4, Bloomsbury Place, London WC1A 2QA
Tel. +44 (020) 7323-5004
Fax +44 (020) 7636-8004

Prestel Publishing
900 Broadway, Suite 603
New York, N.Y. 10003
Tel. +1 (212) 995-2720
Fax +1 (212) 995-2733
www.prestel.com

Library of Congress Control Number: 2005900730

The Deutsche Bibliothek holds a record of this publication in the Deutsche Nationalbibliografie; detailed bibliographical data can be found under: http://dnb.ddb.de

Prestel books are available worldwide. Please contact your nearest bookseller or one of the above addresses for information concerning your local distributor.

Editorial direction by Curt Holtz
Translated by James Roderick O'Donovan, Vienna
Copy-edited by Danko Szabó, Munich
Cover design by LIQUID, Augsburg
Design and layout by Ulrike Schmidt, Andrea Mogwitz
Map design by Barbara Dezasse, Munich
Origination by Repro Ludwig, Zell am See
Printed and bound by Print Consult, Munich

Printed in the EU on acid-free paper
ISBN 3-7913-3135-3